C000100276

NEW MATHS FRAMEWORKING

Matches the revised KS3 Framework

Trevor Senior

ear 6. Workbook

Contents

Exercise 1A   Negative numbers

This exercise will give you practice in

○ reading and writing negative numbers using a number line

1 Write down the numbers that the arrows are pointing to.

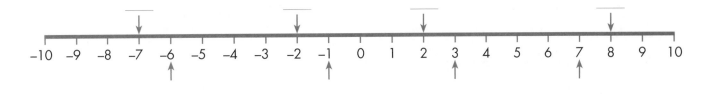

2 Write down the temperatures shown on the thermometer.

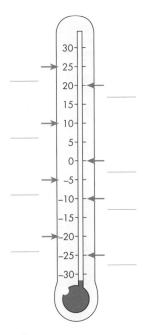

3 Fill in the missing numbers on the number lines below.

a
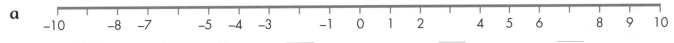

b

c

–20	–16	–12 –10 –8	–4 –2	2 4 6	10 12 14	18 20

d

–100	–80 –70	–40 –30 –20	0 10 20 30	50 60	80 90 100

Exercise 1B   Multiples

This exercise will give you practice in
○ recognising multiples

1 Fill in the missing multiples.

   a Multiples of 2:   2   4   6   ___   ___   ___   ___   ___   ___   ___

   b Multiples of 3:   3   6   9   ___   ___   ___   ___   ___   ___   ___

   c Multiples of 5:   5   10   ___   20   ___   ___   35   ___   ___   ___

   d Multiples of 10:   10   20   ___   ___   50   ___   ___   ___   ___   100

2 Put a circle around the numbers in each row that are multiples of:

a 2	10	4	21	18	27	8	35	15	20
b 3	10	4	21	18	27	8	35	15	20
c 5	10	4	21	18	27	8	35	15	20
d 10	10	4	21	18	27	8	35	15	20

3 Write down the first 10 multiples of:

   a 4   ___ ___ ___ ___ ___ ___ ___ ___

   b 6   ___ ___ ___ ___ ___ ___ ___ ___

   c 7   ___ ___ ___ ___ ___ ___ ___ ___

   d 8   ___ ___ ___ ___ ___ ___ ___ ___

   e 9   ___ ___ ___ ___ ___ ___ ___ ___

4 Put a circle around the numbers in each row that are multiples of:

a 4	12	18	21	24	27	36	49
b 6	12	18	21	24	27	36	49
c 7	12	18	21	24	27	36	49
d 8	12	18	21	24	27	36	49
e 9	12	18	21	24	27	36	49

Exercise 1C   Square numbers

This exercise will give you practice in
- recognising square numbers

1 Complete the following:

a 1 × 1 _____   **b** 2 × 2 _____

c 3 × 3 _____   **d** 4 × 4 _____

e 5 × 5 _____   **f** 6 × 6 _____

g 7 × 7 _____   **h** 8 × 8 _____

i 9 × 9 _____   **j** 10 × 10 _____

k 11 × 11 _____   **l** 12 × 12 _____

2 The answers to question 1 are square numbers.
Use square numbers to make each sum work.
The first one has been done for you.

a 13 = 4 + 9   **b** 5 = 1 + _____

c 8 = 4 + _____   **d** 50 = 1 + _____

e 90 = 81 + _____

f 17 = _____ + _____

g 29 = _____ + _____

h 116 = _____ + _____

3 In parts a, b and c, write down the number of small squares in each diagram.

a _____ small squares

b _____ small squares

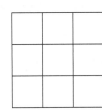

c _____ small squares

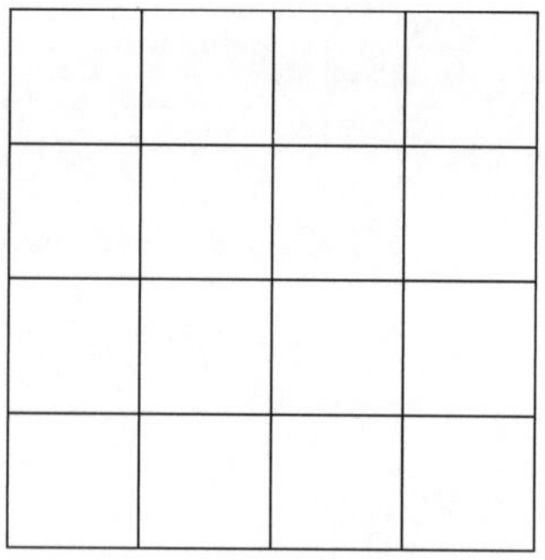

d In the space below, draw the next diagram in the pattern and write down the number of small squares.

_____ small squares

4 The following diagrams show a pattern of squares. Complete the table by counting the number of different sized squares in each diagram.

Exercise 1D   Triangle numbers

This exercise will give you practice in

○ recognising triangle numbers

1 Complete the table of triangle numbers.

	Triangle number
1	1
1 + 2	3
1 + 2 + 3	6
1 + 2 + 3 + 4	
1 + 2 + 3 + 4 + 5	
1 + 2 + 3 + 4 + 5 + 6	
1 + 2 + 3 + 4 + 5 + 6 + 7	
1 + 2 + 3 + 4 + 5 + 6 + 7 + 8	
1 + 2 + 3 + 4 + 5 + 6 + 7 + 8 + 9	
1 + 2 + 3 + 4 + 5 + 6 + 7 + 8 + 9 + 10	

2 **a** Complete the table below by counting the angles in the pattern of diagrams. All of the angles have been marked for you.

Diagram 1   Diagram 2   Diagram 3   Diagram 4

Diagram	1	2	3	4
Number of angles				

b What do you notice?

_____

_____

Exercise 1E Factors

This exercise will give you practice in

● recognising factors

1 Complete the following:

a $3 \times 5 =$ _____ 3 and 5 are factors of 15

b $2 \times 7 =$ _____ 2 and 7 are factors of _____

c $1 \times 6 =$ _____ _____ and _____ are factors of _____

d $8 \times 4 =$ _____ _____ and _____ are factors of _____

e $5 \times$ _____ $= 5$ _____ and _____ are factors of _____

f $6 \times$ _____ $= 18$ _____ and _____ are factors of _____

2 Complete the following:

a $1 \times 9 = 9$ $3 \times 3 = 9$ $9 \times 1 = 9$

The factors of 9 are 1, 3 and _____

b $1 \times$ _____ $= 12$ $2 \times$ _____ $= 12$ $3 \times$ _____ $= 12$

$12 \times$ _____ $= 12$ $6 \times$ _____ $= 12$ $4 \times$ _____ $= 12$

The factors of 12 are _____, _____, _____, _____, _____ and _____

c _____ $\times$ _____ $= 15$ _____ $\times$ _____ $= 15$ _____ $\times$ _____ $= 15$ _____ $\times$ _____ $= 15$

The factors of 15 are _____, _____, _____ and _____

d _____ $\times$ _____ $= 21$ _____ $\times$ _____ $= 21$ _____ $\times$ _____ $= 21$ _____ $\times$ _____ $= 21$

The factors of 21 are _____, _____, _____ and _____

3 Put a circle around the numbers in each row that are factors of:

a 14   1 2 3 4 5 6 7 14

b 16   1 2 3 4 6 8 12 16

c 23   1 2 3 4 6 7 11 23

d 35   1 3 5 7 9 15 30 35

e 40   1 2 4 5 8 10 20 40

f 49   1 2 3 7 14 24 25 49

4 **a**   Find all the factors of 10. ⎯⎯⎯ ⎯⎯⎯ ⎯⎯⎯ ⎯⎯⎯

   b   Find all the factors of 18. ⎯⎯⎯ ⎯⎯⎯ ⎯⎯⎯ ⎯⎯⎯ ⎯⎯⎯ ⎯⎯⎯

   c   Find all the factors of 25. ⎯⎯⎯ ⎯⎯⎯ ⎯⎯⎯

   d   Find all the factors of 30. ⎯⎯⎯ ⎯⎯⎯ ⎯⎯⎯ ⎯⎯⎯ ⎯⎯⎯
   ⎯⎯⎯

   e   Find all the factors of 50. ⎯⎯⎯ ⎯⎯⎯ ⎯⎯⎯ ⎯⎯⎯

   f   Find all the factors of 100. ⎯⎯⎯ ⎯⎯⎯ ⎯⎯⎯ ⎯⎯⎯ ⎯⎯⎯
   ⎯⎯⎯ ⎯⎯⎯

Exercise 1F   Sequences and rules

This exercise will give you practice in

- working out the next terms in a sequence using the term-to-term rule given
- finding the term-to-term rule of a given sequence

1 **a**   Write down the next two terms in each of the sequences given in part **b**.

   b   Write down the term-to-term rule for working out the next number in each sequence.

   i   1, 2, 3, 4, 5, ☐, ☐   The term-to-term rule is ⎯⎯⎯⎯⎯⎯

   ii   1, 3, 5, 7, 9, ☐, ☐   The term-to-term rule is ⎯⎯⎯⎯⎯⎯

   iii 3, 6, 9, 12, 15, ☐, ☐   The term-to-term rule is ⎯⎯⎯⎯⎯⎯

   iv   10, 9, 8, 7, 6, ☐, ☐   The term-to-term rule is ⎯⎯⎯⎯⎯⎯

   v   20, 18, 16, 14, 12, ☐, ☐   The term-to-term rule is ⎯⎯⎯⎯⎯⎯

   vi   100, 95, 90, 85, 80, ☐, ☐   The term-to-term rule is ⎯⎯⎯⎯⎯⎯

   vii 4, 14, 24, 34, 44, ☐, ☐   The term-to-term rule is ⎯⎯⎯⎯⎯⎯

   viii 50, 48, 46, 44, 42, ☐, ☐   The term-to-term rule is ⎯⎯⎯⎯⎯⎯

   ix   3, 2, 1, 0, −1, −2, ☐, ☐   The term-to-term rule is ⎯⎯⎯⎯⎯⎯

   x   −10, −20, −30, −40, −50, ☐, ☐   The term-to-term rule is ⎯⎯⎯⎯⎯⎯

2 Work out the next four terms in each sequence using the term-to-term rule shown.

a   Rule Add 4   3, ☐, ☐, ☐, ☐

b   Rule Subtract 2   19, ☐, ☐, ☐, ☐

c   Rule Add 5   8, ☐, ☐, ☐, ☐

d   Rule Subtract 6   50, ☐, ☐, ☐, ☐

e   Rule Add 7   10, ☐, ☐, ☐, ☐

f   Rule Subtract 10   83, ☐, ☐, ☐, ☐

g   Rule Subtract 4   27, ☐, ☐, ☐, ☐

h   Rule Add 1   −4, ☐, ☐, ☐, ☐

3 a   Write down the next two terms in each of the sequences given in part **b**.

b   Write down the term-to-term rule for working out the next number in each sequence.

i   1, 2, 4, 8, 16, ☐, ☐   The term-to-term rule is _____

ii   1, 10, 100, 1000, 10 000, ☐, ☐   The term-to-term rule is _____

iii 3, 6, 12, 24, 48, ☐, ☐   The term-to-term rule is _____

iv   1 000 000, 100 000, 10 000, 1000, 100, ☐, ☐   The term-to-term rule is _____

v   64, 32, 16, 8, 4, ☐, ☐   The term-to-term rule is _____

4 Work out the next two terms in each sequence using the term-to-term rule shown.

a   Rule Multiply by 2   2, ☐, ☐

b   Rule Divide by 2   20, ☐, ☐

c   Rule Multiply by 10   8, ☐, ☐

d   Rule Divide by 5   25, ☐, ☐

Exercise 1G Term-to-term rules

This exercise will give you practice in
- generating sequences using a term-to-term rule

1 Find the next two numbers in each of the sequences below.

a   2, 4, 6, 8, ☐, ☐

b   3, 5, 7, 9, ☐, ☐

c   10, 20, 30, 40, ☐, ☐

d   10, 9, 8, 7, ☐, ☐

e   7, 10, 13, 16, ☐, ☐

f   15, 18, 21, 24, ☐, ☐

g   17, 15, 13, 11, ☐, ☐

h   23, 28, 33, 38, ☐, ☐

i   3, 9, 15, 21, ☐, ☐

2 Fill in the missing terms for each sequence in the table below.

Term	1st	2nd	3rd	4th	5th	6th	7th	8th	9th	10th
Sequence A					12	13	14	15		
Sequence B		10	12				20			26
Sequence C	4	7		13		19		25		31
Sequence D			15		25		35		45	
Sequence E						36		40		44
Sequence F	21			24						30
Sequence G					13	15	17			
Sequence H				18	22	26				
Sequence I							35	38	41	
Sequence J			45	43	41					
Sequence K						54	50	46		

3 Complete Sequences A–H using the term-to-term rules and starting numbers given.

	Term-to-term rule	1st	2nd	3rd	4th	5th	6th	7th	8th	9th	10th
Sequence A	Add 5	4									
Sequence B	Add 3	3									
Sequence C	Add 2	6									
Sequence D	Add 10	8									
Sequence E	Subtract 3	30									
Sequence F	Subtract 2	25									
Sequence G	Subtract 0.5	10									
Sequence H	Subtract 4	100									

Exercise 1H Real-life sequences

This exercise will give you practice in

- looking at sequences and patterns in real problems

1 In a supermarket, tins are stacked as shown on the right.

   a Write down the number of tins in each row in the spaces provided.

   b If the stack was 100 rows high, how many tins would there be in the bottom row?

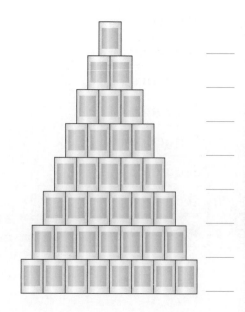

2 The diagram on the right shows a pattern made from posts and rails.

Pattern 1

Pattern 2

Pattern 3

a   Draw the next diagram in the pattern.

b   Complete the table to show the number of posts and rails in each pattern.

c   How many posts will be in Pattern 5?

_____

d   How many rails will be in Pattern 5?

_____

Pattern	1	2	3	4
Number of posts	2	3	4	5
Number of rails	3			

3 The diagram on the right shows a pattern of tables and chairs.

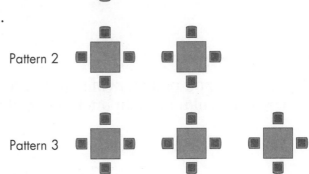

Pattern 1

Pattern 2

Pattern 3

a   Complete the table below to show the number of tables and chairs in each pattern.

Pattern	1	2	3	4
Number of tables	1	2	3	4
Number of chairs	4			

b   How many chairs will be in Pattern 5?

_____

4 The diagram on the right shows a pattern of sticks.

Diagram 1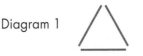

a   Complete the table below to show the number of sticks in each diagram.

Diagram 2

Pattern	1	2	3	4
Number of sticks	3	5		

b   How many sticks will be in Pattern 5?

Diagram 3

_____

Exercise 2A Lines

This exercise will give you practice in

o recognising parallel, perpendicular (at right angles), horizontal and vertical lines

1. Write the letter V next to any vertical lines and the letter H next to any horizontal lines.

a    b   c   d   e    f

g    h   i   j 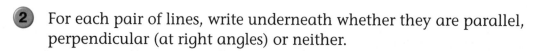   k

2. For each pair of lines, write underneath whether they are parallel, perpendicular (at right angles) or neither.

a    b    c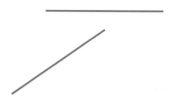

d    e    f

3 **a** For each line below, draw a second line that is **parallel** to the given line.

 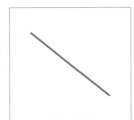 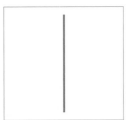 

b For each line below, draw a second line that is **perpendicular** (at right angles) to the given line.

 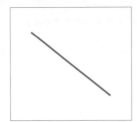 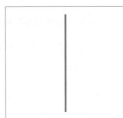 

c For each line below, draw a second line that is **neither parallel nor perpendicular** (at right angles) to the given line.

Exercise 2B Classifying and ordering angles

This exercise will give you practice in
- recognising acute, obtuse and reflex angles

1 Write down whether each angle shown is acute, obtuse or reflex.

a **b** **c** **d**

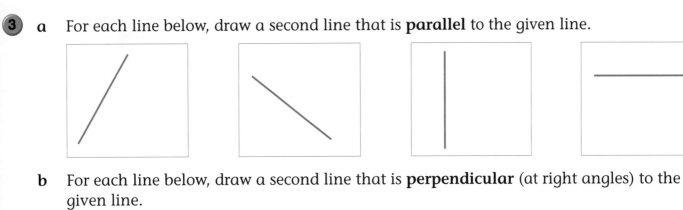

e **f** **g** **h**

 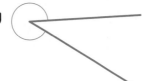 

2 Label the ten angles below from 1 to 10 starting with the smallest first.

a    b    c    d 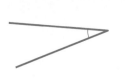   e

f    g   h    i   j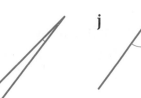

Exercise 2C Calculating angles on a straight line

This exercise will give you practice in

○ calculating the missing angle on a straight line using your knowledge that angles on a straight line add up to 180°

1 Find the missing angle on each straight line by filling in the answers to the calculations.

a 180° − 170° = _____

b 180° − 40° = _____

c 180° − 160° = _____

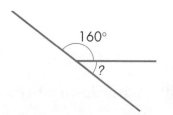

d 180° − 90° = _____

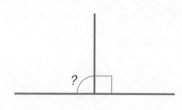

e 180° − 120° = _____

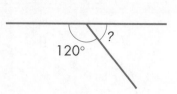

f 180° − 30° = _____

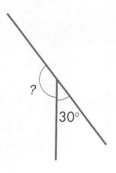

g 90° + 60° = _____

180° – _____ = _____

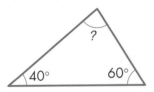

h 70° + 30° = _____

180° – _____ = _____

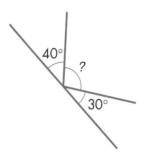

i 40° + 30° = _____

180° – _____ = _____

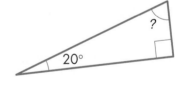

Exercise 2D Calculating angles in triangles

This exercise will give you practice in

o calculating the missing angle in a triangle using your knowledge that the angles in a triangle add up to 180°

1 Find the missing angle in each of the triangles below by filling in the answers to the calculations.

a 40° + 60° = _____

180° – _____ = _____

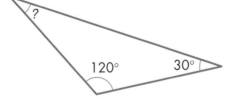

b 120° + 30° = _____

180° – _____ = _____

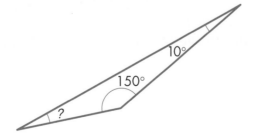

c 90° + 20° = _____

180° – _____ = _____

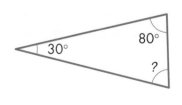

d 70° + 70° = _____

180° – _____ = _____

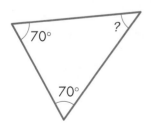

e 10° + 150° = _____

180° – _____ = _____

f 30° + 80° = _____

180° – _____ = _____

g 60° + 50° = _____

180° – _____ = _____

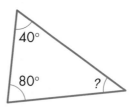

h 80° + 40° = _____

180° – _____ = _____

i 120° + 30° = _____

180° – _____ = _____

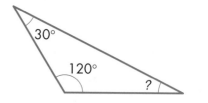

Exercise 2E 2-D shapes

> **This exercise will give you practice in**
> ○ recognising 2-D shapes

1 Label each of the following shapes with the correct mathematical name.

> Delta (Arrowhead)   Pentagon   Kite   Rhombus   Hexagon
> Parallelogram   Trapezium   Rectangle   Triangle   Square

a    **b**   **c**   **d** 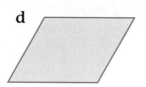   **e**

_____   _____   _____   _____   _____

f 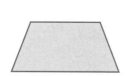   **g**    **h**    **i**   **j**

_____   _____   _____   _____   _____

2 Label each of the following shapes with the correct mathematical name.

> Scalene triangle   Right-angled triangle   Equilateral triangle   Isosceles triangle

a   **b**   **c**    **d**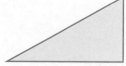

_____   _____   _____   _____

3 Draw each of the following shapes onto the dotty grid.

a   Rectangle   **b**   Isosceles triangle   **c**   Right-angled triangle

d   Parallelogram   **e**   Kite

4 Look at each of the flags below and write down any shapes that you can see.

a

b

c

d

e

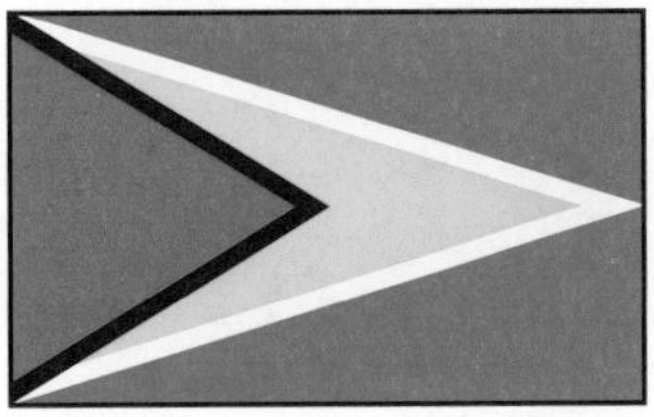

f

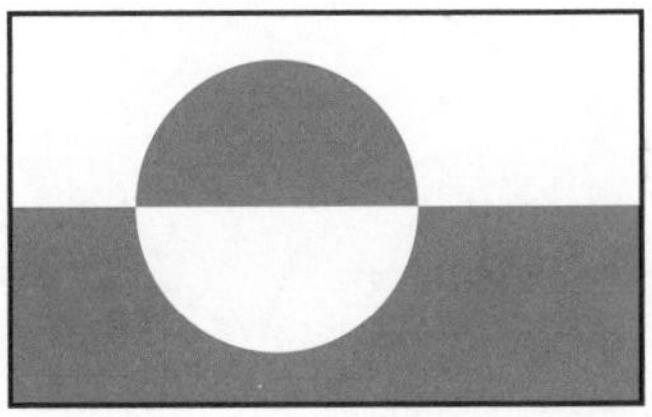

Exercise 2F Measuring angles

This exercise will give you practice in

○ measuring acute and obtuse angles

① Use the protractor to measure each of the following acute angles. Write your answer beside the angle.

a

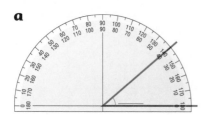

b

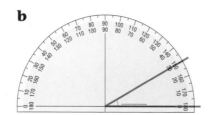

c

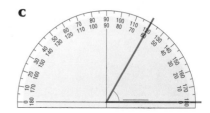

d

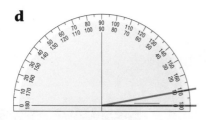

e

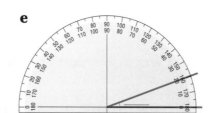

f

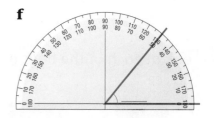

② Use the protractor to measure each of the following obtuse angles. Write your answer beside the angle.

a

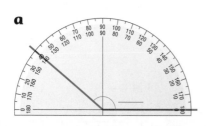

b

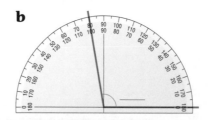

c

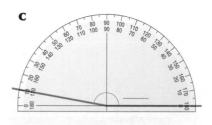

d

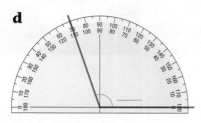

e

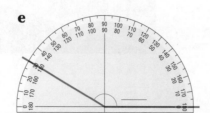

f

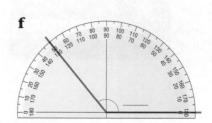

Exercise 3A Chance

This exercise will give you practice in

- using the vocabulary of chance

Impossible   Very unlikely   Unlikely   Evens   Likely   Very likely   Certain

1. Write each of the statements below in the correct box.

50–50 chance   Good chance
No chance   Poor chance
Even chance   Definitely will happen
Will probably happen   Definitely will not happen
Low chance   Very poor chance
Very doubtful   Doubtful
High chance   Equal chance
Almost certain to happen   Very good chance
Almost impossible

Impossible	**Very unlikely**

Unlikely	**Evens**

Likely	Very likely

Certain

2 Choose one of the following words to describe the chance of each of the following events occurring.

Impossible   Very unlikely   Unlikely   Evens   Likely   Very likely   Certain

a   It will snow in London in July.   _____

b   The postman will deliver a letter to my house today.   _____

c   The next car I see will be purple.   _____

d   The person nearest to me is using a blue pen.   _____

e   The next person to walk in the room will be male.   _____

f   You will get a 6 when you throw a dice.   _____

g   You will watch TV tonight.   _____

3 Make up your own list of events for each of the following probabilities.

Impossible	Unlikely	Evens

Likely	Certain

Exercise 3B   Calculating chance

This exercise will give you practice in
- working out the chance of an event happening and showing your answer on a scale.

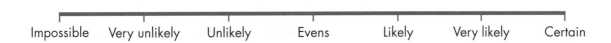 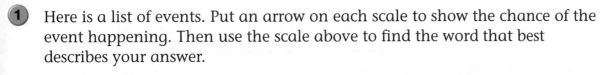
Impossible   Very unlikely   Unlikely   Evens   Likely   Very likely   Certain

1 Here is a list of events. Put an arrow on each scale to show the chance of the event happening. Then use the scale above to find the word that best describes your answer.

a You will get a head if you flip a fair coin.

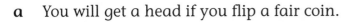
Impossible   Certain

b You will get a 6 if you roll a fair dice.

Impossible   Certain

c You will get a 1 or a 2 if you roll a fair dice.

Impossible   Certain

d You will get an even number if you roll a fair dice.

Impossible   Certain

e You will get a number less than 6 if you roll a fair dice.

Impossible   Certain

f You will pick a red disc out of a bag containing 5 blue discs and no red discs.

Impossible   Certain

g You will pick a red disc out of a bag containing 2 blue discs and 3 red discs.

Impossible   Certain

h You will pick a red disc out of a bag containing no blue discs and 5 red discs.

Impossible   Certain

---

2 Each bag contains 10 marbles. Put an arrow on each scale to show the chance of picking a red marble from each bag.

a 1 red and 9 blue

Impossible   Certain

b 2 red and 8 blue

Impossible   Certain

c 4 red and 6 blue

Impossible   Certain

d 7 red and 3 blue

Impossible   Certain

e 10 red and 0 blue

Impossible   Certain

f 6 red and 4 blue

Impossible   Certain

g 0 red and 10 blue

Impossible   Certain

h 8 red and 2 blue

Impossible   Certain

i 5 red and 5 blue

Impossible   Certain

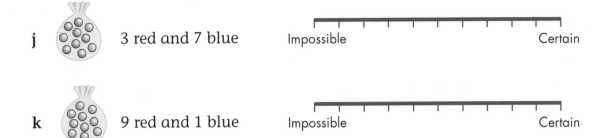

j 3 red and 7 blue   Impossible   Certain

k 9 red and 1 blue   Impossible   Certain

Exercise 3C   Reading data from frequency tables

This exercise will give you practice in

- solving problems by reading information from a frequency table

1 The frequency table on the right shows the destinations of aeroplanes from a UK airport.

Airport destinations	Frequency
Spain	18
USA	8
Canary Islands	25
Other	20
Total	71

    a   How many aeroplanes went to the USA?

      _____

    b   Which destination had the most planes?

      _____

    c   How many more planes departed to Spain than to the USA? _____

2 The table on the right shows the number of times students in a class are absent on each weekday.

	Number of absences
Monday	17
Tuesday	12
Wednesday	6
Thursday	11
Friday	18
Total	64

    a   On which day of the week were there most absences?

      _____

    b   On which day of the week were there least absences?

      _____

    c   How many more absences were there on Friday than on Thursday? _____

3 Thirty students were asked what they enjoy doing in their spare time. Their answers are given in the table on the right.

	Number of students
Texting	5
Sport	8
Watching TV	4
Reading	4
Going out	9
Total	30

a   What was the most popular answer?

_____

b   How many students did not say 'Going out'?

_____

c   Matt thinks that over half picked 'Going out' or 'Sport'. Is he correct? _____

Explain how you know. _____

_____

4 The table on the right shows the pets owned by a class of Year 8 students.

Pet	Frequency
Dog	12
Cat	9
Snake	1
Hamster	4
Fish	5
Other	7

a   How many pets were owned altogether?

_____

b   How many more dogs were owned than cats?

_____

c   Complete the sentences below.

   i   There are three times as many _____ as there are _____.

   ii   The number of cats + the number of hamsters = the number of dogs + the number

   of _____.

Exercise 4A Fractions

This exercise will give you practice in

○ recognising fractions of different shapes and quantities

1 What fraction of each shape is shaded?

a  _____

b _____

c _____

d 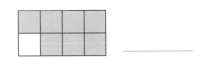 _____

e _____

f  _____

g 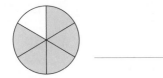 _____

h  _____

i _____

2 a Colour in $\frac{1}{3}$ of the bottles.

b Colour in $\frac{3}{4}$ of the pens.

c Colour in $\frac{1}{5}$ of the cars.

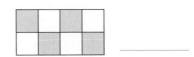

d Colour in $\frac{2}{3}$ of the phones.

e Colour in $\frac{3}{5}$ of the houses.

f Colour in $\frac{1}{4}$ of the light bulbs.

Exercise 4B Equivalent fractions

This exercise will give you practice in
- cancelling down fractions
- recognising equivalent fractions

1 Fill in the missing numbers to complete the equivalent fractions for each of the shapes below.

a $\dfrac{3}{\underline{}} = \dfrac{}{2}$

b 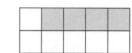 $\dfrac{4}{\underline{}} = \dfrac{}{5}$

c $\dfrac{}{8} = \dfrac{3}{\underline{}}$

d $\dfrac{}{6} = \dfrac{2}{\underline{}}$

2 Fill in the missing numbers in each of these equivalent fractions.

a $\dfrac{4}{8} = \dfrac{}{2}$

b $\dfrac{3}{15} = \dfrac{}{5}$

c $\dfrac{6}{8} = \dfrac{}{4}$

d $\dfrac{4}{12} = \dfrac{}{3}$

e $\dfrac{10}{20} = \dfrac{}{2}$

3 Join up each pair of equivalent fractions with a line.

$\dfrac{4}{5}$ $\dfrac{15}{20}$ $\dfrac{6}{12}$

$\dfrac{1}{2}$ $\dfrac{8}{10}$ $\dfrac{2}{3}$

$\dfrac{4}{6}$ $\dfrac{3}{4}$

Exercise 4C Adding and subtracting fractions

This exercise will give you practice in
- adding and subtracting fractions

1 Complete each of these fraction statements. Part **a** has been done for you.

a + 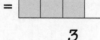 =

$\dfrac{1}{5}$ + $\dfrac{2}{5}$ = $\dfrac{3}{5}$

b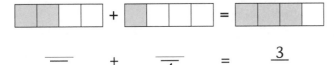

$$\frac{}{7} \quad + \quad \frac{3}{7} \quad = \quad \frac{}{7}$$

c

$$\frac{}{} \quad + \quad \frac{}{4} \quad = \quad \frac{3}{}$$

d

$$\frac{3}{} \quad + \quad \frac{}{} \quad = \quad \frac{7}{8}$$

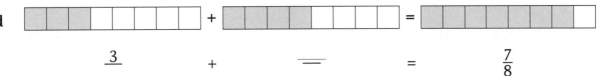

2 Fill in the gaps to add the following fractions and give your answer in its simplest form.

a $\frac{1}{5} + \frac{3}{5} = \frac{}{5}$

b $\frac{2}{7} + \frac{3}{7} = \frac{}{7}$

c $\frac{1}{9} + \frac{4}{9} = \frac{}{}$

d $\frac{3}{10} + \frac{2}{10} = \frac{}{10} = \frac{1}{2}$

e $\frac{1}{4} + \frac{1}{2} = \frac{1}{4} + \frac{}{4} = \frac{}{4}$

f $\frac{3}{10} + \frac{1}{2} = \frac{3}{10} + \frac{}{10} = \frac{}{10} = \frac{}{5}$

g $\frac{1}{8} + \frac{1}{4} = \frac{1}{8} + \frac{}{8} = \frac{}{8}$

h $\frac{1}{2} + \frac{1}{3} = \frac{}{6} + \frac{}{6} = \frac{}{6}$

3 Fill in the gaps to subtract the following fractions and give the answer in its simplest form.

a $\frac{7}{9} - \frac{2}{9} = \frac{}{9}$

b $\frac{4}{7} - \frac{3}{7} = \frac{}{7}$

c $\frac{5}{11} - \frac{2}{11} = \frac{}{}$

d $\frac{7}{10} - \frac{2}{10} = \frac{}{10} = \frac{}{2}$

e $\frac{17}{20} - \frac{7}{20} = \frac{}{20} = \frac{}{2}$

f $\frac{9}{10} - \frac{4}{5} = \frac{9}{10} - \frac{}{10} = \frac{}{10}$

g $\frac{7}{8} - \frac{1}{4} = \frac{7}{8} - \frac{}{8} = \frac{}{8}$

h $\frac{11}{12} - \frac{5}{6} = \frac{11}{12} - \frac{}{12} = \frac{}{12}$

Exercise 4D Fractions of quantities

This exercise will give you practice in
- working out fractions of quantities

1 Work out each of the following.

a $\frac{1}{2}$ of 20 = _____

b $\frac{1}{3}$ of 12 = _____

c $\frac{1}{4}$ of 24 = _____

d $\frac{1}{2}$ of 44 = _____

e $\frac{1}{3}$ of 30 = _____

f $\frac{1}{4}$ of 32 = _____

g $\frac{1}{5}$ of 25 = _____

h $\frac{1}{10}$ of 40 = _____

i $\frac{1}{5}$ of 45 = _____

j $\frac{1}{4}$ of 36 = _____

k $\frac{1}{6}$ of 30 = _____

l $\frac{1}{8}$ of 32 = _____

2 Work out each of the following.

a $\frac{2}{3}$ of 12 = _____

b $\frac{3}{4}$ of 24 = _____

c $\frac{2}{3}$ of 30 = _____

d $\frac{3}{4}$ of 32 = _____

e $\frac{2}{5}$ of 25 = _____

f $\frac{4}{5}$ of 25 = _____

g $\frac{3}{10}$ of 40 = _____

h $\frac{7}{10}$ of 40 = _____

i $\frac{3}{5}$ of 45 = _____

j $\frac{3}{4}$ of 36 = _____

k $\frac{5}{6}$ of 30 = _____

l $\frac{3}{8}$ of 32 = _____

Exercise 4E   Percentages, fractions and decimals

This exercise will give you practice in

○ understanding percentages as parts of a hundred

1 Complete each of these statements.

a   60% is equivalent to $\frac{}{100}$, _____% is equivalent to 0.60

b   20% is equivalent to $\frac{}{100}$,   20% is equivalent to _____

c   25% is equivalent to $\frac{}{100}$,   25% is equivalent to _____

d   75% is equivalent to $\frac{}{100}$, _____ is equivalent to 0.75

e   10% is equivalent to $\frac{}{100}$,   10% is equivalent to _____

f   30% is equivalent to $\frac{}{100}$,   30% is equivalent to _____

g   80% is equivalent to $\frac{}{100}$, _____ is equivalent to 0.80

h   50% is equivalent to $\frac{}{100}$,   50% is equivalent to _____

2 Here are some percentages and some fractions. Join up the ones which have the same value.

10%   75%
    25%
 	
   90%
50%
    20%
	$\frac{1}{5}$ $\frac{1}{2}$ $\frac{1}{4}$
	
	   $\frac{9}{10}$ $\frac{1}{10}$ $\frac{3}{4}$

3 Here are some percentages and some decimals. Join up the ones which have the same value.

10%   75%
   90%   25%
      40%
50%   80%
   20%
	0.9
	    0.5 0.4
	
	   0.75 0.25 0.2
	    0.1
	      0.8

Exercise 5A Finding unknown numbers

This exercise will give you practice in

- finding missing numbers in additions, subtractions, multiplications and divisions

1 Fill in the boxes to make each addition calculation correct.

    a $5 + 6 = \boxed{}$ **b** $11 + 23 = \boxed{}$ **c** $5 + \boxed{} = 12$

    d $\boxed{} + 3 = 9$ **e** $\boxed{} + 12 = 15$ **f** $8 + \boxed{} = 13$

2 Fill in the spaces to make each subtraction correct.

    a $7 - 3 = \boxed{}$ **b** $10 - 6 = \boxed{}$ **c** $8 - \boxed{} = 3$

    d $7 - \boxed{} = 7$ **e** $12 - \boxed{} = 4$ **f** $10 - \boxed{} = 5$

3 Fill in the boxes to make each multiplication correct.

    a $3 \times 5 = \boxed{}$ **b** $6 \times 3 = \boxed{}$ **c** $5 \times \boxed{} = 20$

    d $\boxed{} \times 2 = 12$ **e** $\boxed{} \times 4 = 16$ **f** $8 \times \boxed{} = 16$

4 Fill in the spaces to make each division correct.

    a $10 \div 2 = \boxed{}$ **b** $15 \div 3 = \boxed{}$ **c** $10 \div \boxed{} = 2$

    d $20 \div \boxed{} = 5$ **e** $\boxed{} \div 3 = 7$ **f** $\boxed{} \div 4 = 5$

5 Write down the different pairs of numbers that could go in the empty boxes to make each of these calculations correct.

a 　□ + □ = 7　　□ + □ = 7　　□ + □ = 7　　□ + □ = 7　　□ + □ = 7

　□ + □ = 7　　□ + □ = 7　　□ + □ = 7

b 　□ + □ = 4　　□ + □ = 4　　□ + □ = 4　　□ + □ = 4　　□ + □ = 4

c 　□ × □ = 12　　□ × □ = 12　　□ × □ = 12　　□ × □ = 12　　□ × □ = 12

　□ × □ = 12

d 　□ × □ = 10　　□ × □ = 10　　□ × □ = 10　　□ × □ = 10

Exercise 5B　Introducing expressions

This exercise will give you practice in

○ writing down word sentences using letter symbols

1 Put a circle around all of the expressions that are the same as $3n$.

$$n + n + n \qquad 3n \qquad 2n + n \qquad n \times 3 \qquad 3 \times n$$

$$n + 2n \qquad n \times n \times n \qquad 3 + n \qquad n + 3$$

2 Join up the expressions that are the same.

$$n + n \qquad n + 2 \qquad 2n \qquad 2 + n \qquad n \div 2 \qquad \tfrac{1}{2}n$$

3 Complete the table below. The first one has been done for you.

Word sentence	Expression using n
Add 7 to a number	$n + 7$
Add 5 to a number	
	$n + 10$
Subtract 4 from a number	
	$n - 3$
5 minus a number	
	$n - 1$
A number multiplied by 2	
	$3n$
A number divided by 4	
	$n \div 2$
	$\frac{1}{2}n$
6 divided by a number	
	$10 \div n$

Exercise 5C   Like terms

This exercise will give you practice in
- collecting like terms

1 Simplify each of the following expressions.

a $a + a + a$ _____

b $2b + 3b$ _____

c $c + 3c$ _____

d $4d - 2d$ _____

e $3e + e - 2e$ _____

f $5f - 3f + 2f$ _____

g $3g - 2g + 3g$ _____

h $2a + 3a + 4b - b$ _____

i $4c - 3c + 2d - d$ _____

j $2e - 3e$ _____

k $4f - 6f$ _____

l $5g + 2g + 3h - 5h$ _____

2 Draw a line to match up the equivalent expressions. The first one has been done for you.

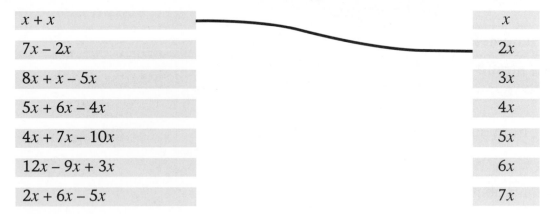

$x + x$	x
$7x - 2x$	$2x$
$8x + x - 5x$	$3x$
$5x + 6x - 4x$	$4x$
$4x + 7x - 10x$	$5x$
$12x - 9x + 3x$	$6x$
$2x + 6x - 5x$	$7x$

3 Write down the perimeter of each of the following shapes as simply as possible.

a **b** **c** **d** **e**

  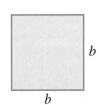 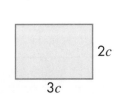 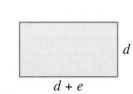 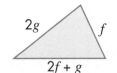

_____ _____ _____ _____ _____

Exercise 5D Solving 'brick wall' problems

This exercise will give you practice in

○ solving problems using 'brick walls'

1 Complete each of the following 'brick walls'. Add the numbers on the two 'bricks' next to each other to give the number in the 'brick' above them.

a **b** **c**

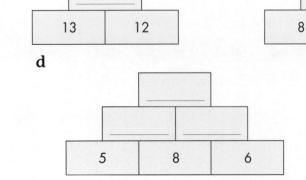 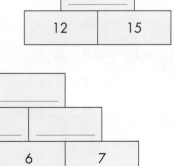

d **e**

2 Complete each of the following 'brick walls'. Add the letters on the two 'bricks' next to each other to give the answer in the 'brick' above them.

a   **b**   **c**   **d**

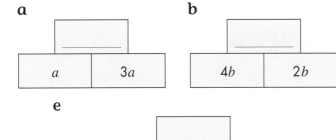

a	$3a$

$4b$	$2b$

$3e - f$	$e + 2f$

$g + h$	$g - h$

e   **f**

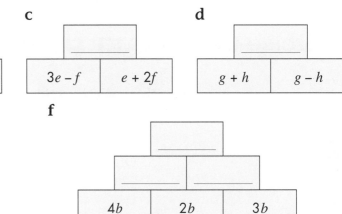

a	$3a$	$5a$

$4b$	$2b$	$3b$

3 Complete each of the following 'brick walls'. Make sure that the 'bricks' next to each other add up to the 'brick' above them.

a   **b**   **c**   **d**

$5a$	
$2a$	

$6b$	
	$4b$

$3c + 4d$	
$c + 3d$	

$6c - d$	
	$3c - d$

e   **f**   **g**

	$4a$	
a		a

$3b$		
	$2b$	$6b$

$c + d$	$c + 2d$	
	d	

4 For each of the following 'brick walls', work out the value of x.

a   **b**   **c**   **d**

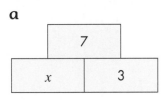
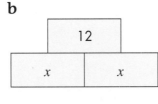
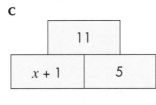
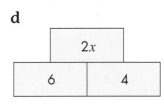

7	
x	3

12	
x	x

11	
$x + 1$	5

$2x$	
6	4

$x =$ _____ $x =$ _____ $x =$ _____ $x =$ _____

Exercise 6A Area of rectangles

This exercise will give you practice in

- working out the area of a rectangle using a counting method
- working out the area of simple compound shapes

1 Work out the area of each of these rectangles. Each square represents 1 square centimetre.

a

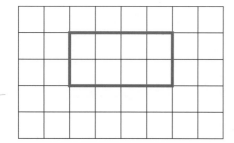

Area = _____ cm^2

b

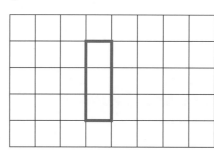

Area = _____ cm^2

c

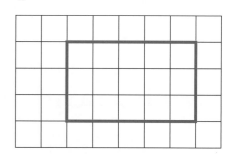

Area = _____ cm^2

2 Find the area of each of the rectangles below.

a

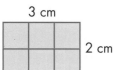

3 cm

2 cm

Area = _____

= _____ cm^2

b

4 cm

1 cm

Area = _____

= _____ cm^2

c

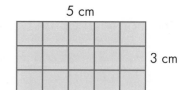

5 cm

3 cm

Area = _____

= _____ cm^2

3 Use the square grid to complete the table for Rectangles A to F.

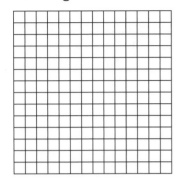

Rectangle	Length	Width	Area
A	3 cm	4 cm	_____ cm²
B	5 cm	2 cm	_____ _____
C	8 m	3 m	_____ m²
D	6 m	4 m	_____ _____
E	10 cm	8 cm	_____ _____
F	9 m	4 m	_____ _____

4 A path is a T shape made of two identical rectangles, as shown on the right. Work out the total area of the path.

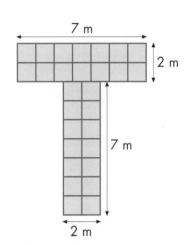

7 m

2 m

7 m

2 m

_____

_____

_____

_____

Exercise 6B Perimeter of rectangles

This exercise will give you practice in

- working out the perimeter of a rectangle using a counting method

1 Work out the perimeter of each of these rectangles. Each square represents 1 square centimetre.

a

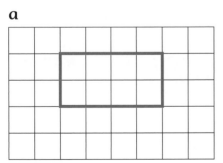

b

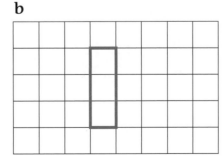

c

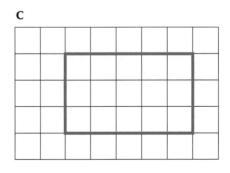

Perimeter = _____ cm   Perimeter = _____ cm   Perimeter = _____ cm

2 Work out the perimeter of each of these shapes. Each square represents 1 square centimetre.

a

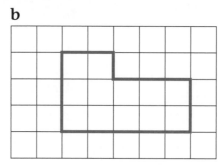

b

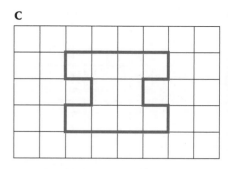

c

Perimeter = _____ cm   Perimeter = _____ cm   Perimeter = _____ cm

3 Find the perimeter of each of the rectangles below.

a   3 cm

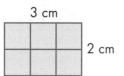

2 cm

Perimeter = _____

= _____ cm

b   4 cm

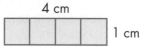

1 cm

Perimeter = _____

= _____ cm

c   5 cm

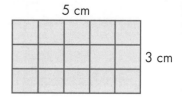

3 cm

Perimeter = _____

= _____ cm

d   6 cm

2 cm

Perimeter = _____

= _____ cm

e   8 cm

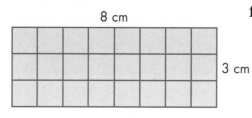

3 cm

Perimeter = _____

= _____ cm

f   4 cm

5 cm

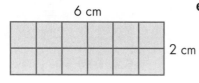

Perimeter = _____

= _____ cm

4 Complete the table for Rectangles A to F.

Rectangle	Length	Width	Perimeter
A	3 cm	4 cm	_____ cm
B	5 cm	2 cm	_____ _____
C	8 m	3 m	_____ m
D	6 m	4 m	_____ _____
E	10 cm	8 cm	_____ _____
F	9 m	4 m	_____ _____

5 A school sports field is 25 metres long and 40 metres wide. Work out the perimeter of the field.

Exercise 6C Reading scales

This exercise will give you practice in
- reading scales on a range of measuring instruments

1 Write down the amount shown on each diagram in the space provided. Don't forget the units.

a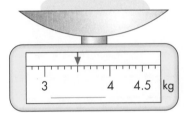

b

c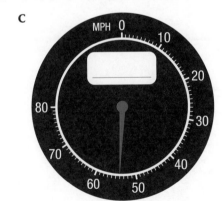

d

e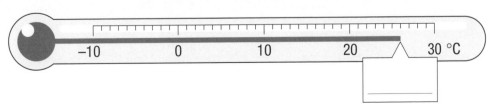

f

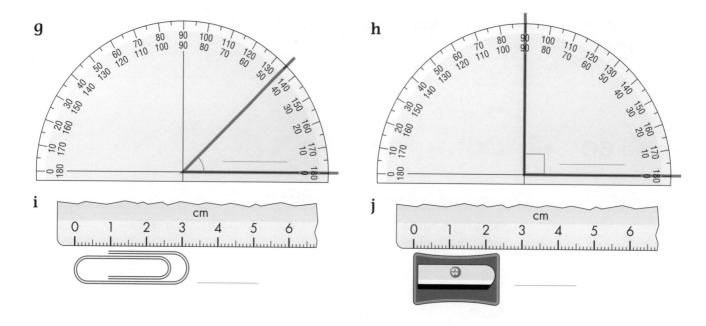

g

h

i

cm

j

cm

2 Write down the mass shown on each of the following scales.

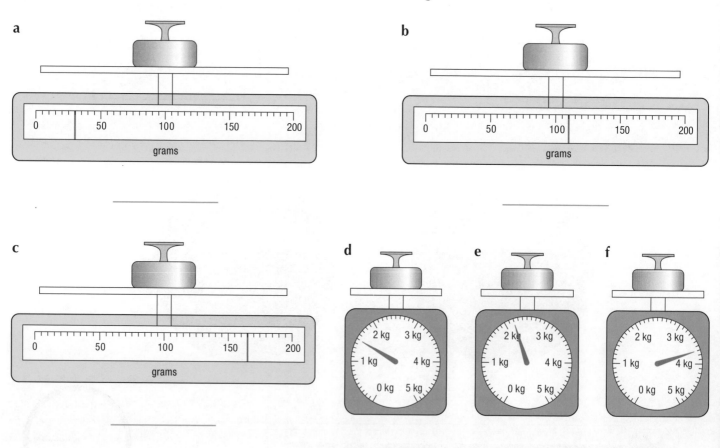

a

b

c

d

e

f

3 Write down the volume of water in each of the following jugs.

a

b

c

d

Exercise 6D Metric units

This exercise will give you practice in
- converting metric units of length
- ordering metric units of mass and capacity

1 Complete each of the following by writing in the missing numbers.

1 centimetre (cm) = 10 millimetres (mm)

a   5 cm = 5 × 10 mm = _____ mm

b   17 cm = 17 × 10 mm = _____ mm

c   9 cm = 9 × _____ mm = _____ mm

d   35 cm = 35 × _____ mm = _____ mm

e   7.8 cm = 7.8 × _____ mm = _____ mm

f   20 mm = 20 ÷ 10 cm = _____ cm

g   310 mm = 310 ÷ _____ cm = _____ cm

h   60 mm = 60 ÷ _____ cm = _____ cm

i   45 mm = 45 ÷ _____ cm = _____ cm

2 Complete each of the following by writing in the missing numbers.

1 metre (m) = 100 centimetres (cm)

a   6 m = 6 × 100 cm = _____ cm

b   13 m = 13 × 100 cm = _____ cm

c   10 m = 10 × _____ cm = _____ cm

d   25 m = 25 × _____ cm = _____ cm

e   6.1 m = 6.1 × _____ cm = _____ cm

f   300 cm = 300 ÷ 100 m = _____ m

g   460 cm = 460 ÷ _____ m = _____ m

h   60 cm = 60 ÷ _____ m = _____ m

i   85 mm = 85 ÷ _____ m = _____ m

3 Complete each of the following by writing in the missing numbers.

> 1 kilometre (km) = 1000 metres (m)

a   2 km = 2 × 1000 m = _____ m

b   11 km = 11 × 1000 m = _____ m

c   20 km = 20 × _____ m = _____ m

d   41 km = 41 × _____ m = _____ m

e   3.4 km = 3.4 × _____ m = _____ m

f   5000 m = 5000 ÷ 1000 km = _____ km

g   6300 m = 6300 ÷ _____ km = _____ km

h   250 m = 250 ÷ _____ km = _____ km

i   125 m = 125 ÷ _____ km = _____ km

4 Complete parts **a** and **b** of the following by writing in the missing numbers.

> 1 kilogram (kg) = 1000 grams (g)

a   25 kg = 25 × 1000 g = _____ g

b   2.5 kg = 2.5 × _____ g = _____ g

c   Number the following bags from 1 to 5 in order of size, starting with the smallest.

25 g   2.5 kg   250 g   25 kg   0.25 g

_____   _____   _____   _____   _____

5 Match the labels to the correct bottles using their relative size.

> 1 litre (l) = 1000 millilitres (ml)
> 1 centilitre (cl) = 10 millilitres (ml)
> 1 litre (l) = 100 centilitres

2 litres

100 ml

150 cl

1 litre

70 cl

Exercise 7A Function machines

This exercise will give you practice in
- using function machines

1 Fill in the missing outputs for each function machine below.

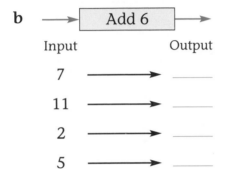

a → Add 3 →

Input	Output
4	_____
5	_____
8	_____
10	_____

b → Add 6 →

Input	Output
7	_____
11	_____
2	_____
5	_____

c → Add 10 →

Input	Output
13	_____
4	_____
25	_____
37	_____

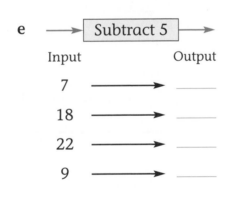

d → Subtract 4 →

Input	Output
10	_____
5	_____
7	_____
23	_____

e → Subtract 5 →

Input	Output
7	_____
18	_____
22	_____
9	_____

f → Subtract 10 →

Input	Output
84	_____
22	_____
35	_____
27	_____

2 Fill in the missing outputs for each function machine below.

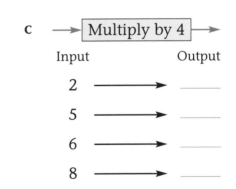

a → Multiply by 2 →

Input	Output
4	_____
6	_____
10	_____
22	_____

b → Multiply by 5 →

Input	Output
3	_____
5	_____
6	_____
10	_____

c → Multiply by 4 →

Input	Output
2	_____
5	_____
6	_____
8	_____

d → Divide by 2 →   **e** → Divide by 5 →   **f** → Divide by 4 →

Input	Output		Input	Output		Input	Output
4 → ___			10 → ___			8 → ___	
6 → ___			15 → ___			12 → ___	
8 → ___			25 → ___			20 → ___	
20 → ___			50 → ___			40 → ___	

(3) Fill in each function machine box with a rule that works. For parts **e–g**, try to fill in each box with a different rule.

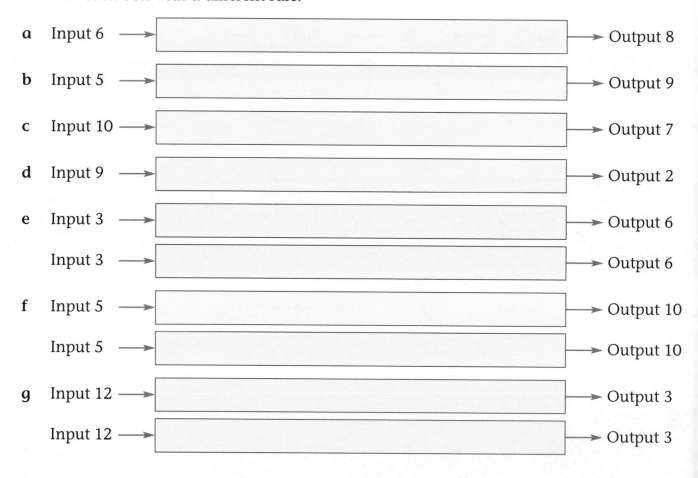

a   Input 6 → [   ] → Output 8

b   Input 5 → [   ] → Output 9

c   Input 10 → [   ] → Output 7

d   Input 9 → [   ] → Output 2

e   Input 3 → [   ] → Output 6

    Input 3 → [   ] → Output 6

f   Input 5 → [   ] → Output 10

    Input 5 → [   ] → Output 10

g   Input 12 → [   ] → Output 3

    Input 12 → [   ] → Output 3

Exercise 7B   Using letter symbols to represent functions

This exercise will give you practice in

○ using letters to explain a rule

1 Fill in the missing outputs for each function machine below.

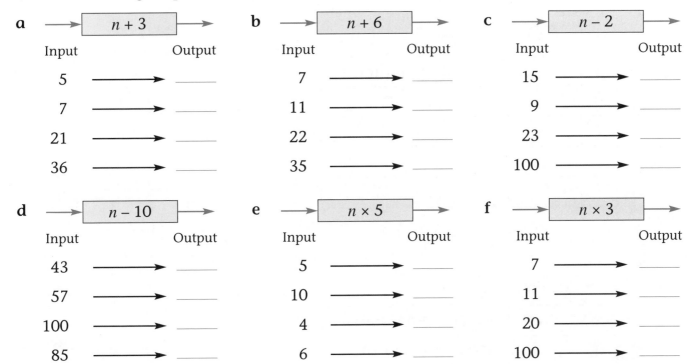

a   → [$n + 3$] →

Input	Output
5	——
7	——
21	——
36	——

b   → [$n + 6$] →

Input	Output
7	——
11	——
22	——
35	——

c   → [$n - 2$] →

Input	Output
15	——
9	——
23	——
100	——

d   → [$n - 10$] →

Input	Output
43	——
57	——
100	——
85	——

e   → [$n \times 5$] →

Input	Output
5	——
10	——
4	——
6	——

f   → [$n \times 3$] →

Input	Output
7	——
11	——
20	——
100	——

2 Write down a function machine rule for each of the following using the letter n. For part **e**, try to find two different rules.

a Input 3 → [   ] → Output 5

b Input 5 → [   ] → Output 8

c Input 10 → [   ] → Output 9

d Input 9 → [   ] → Output 7

e Input 2 → [   ] → Output 4

Input 2 → [   ] → Output 4

45

Exercise 7C   Straight-line graphs

This exercise will give you practice in

- following a rule and drawing straight lines on a graph

① Complete each of the following tables and plot the points on the grid. Join the points with a ruled line.

a $y = x + 2$

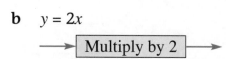

x	→	y = x + 2	Coordinates
0		2	(0, 2)
1		3	(1, 3)
2			
3			

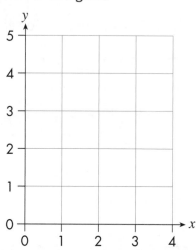

b $y = 2x$

Multiply by 2

x	→	y = 2x	Coordinates
0		0	(0, 0)
1		2	(1, 2)
2			
3			

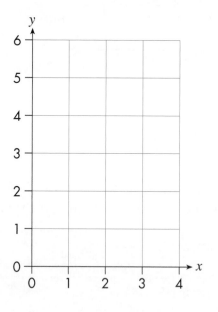

c $y = x + 1$

Add 1

x	→	y = x + 1	Coordinates
0		1	(0, 1)
1			(1, ____)
2			
3			

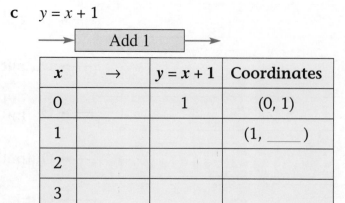

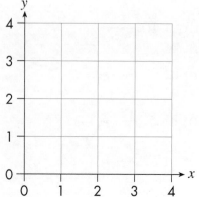

d $y = 3x$

→ Multiply by 3 →

x	$\rightarrow$	$y = 3x$	Coordinates
0		0	(0, 0)
1			(1, ____)
2			
3			

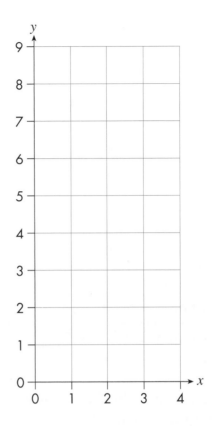

e $y = 2x + 1$

→ Multiply by 2 → Add 1 →

x	$\rightarrow$	$y = 2x + 1$	Coordinates
0		1	(0, 1)
1			(1, ____)
2			
3			

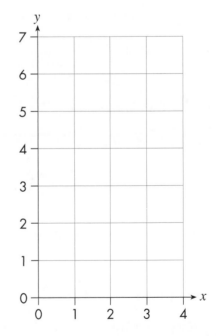

Exercise 8A Decimals and place value

This exercise will give you practice in

○ understanding decimals and place value

1 Complete the table below by writing down the value of the 6 in each number. Two have been done for you.

Number	164	6094	2654	906	161.5	24.63	81.36	105.65	192.86
Value of the 6	60					$\frac{6}{10}$			

2 Complete the table below by writing down the value of the 4 in each number. Two have been done for you.

Number	413	9415	794	940	834.1	20.04	87.49	639.64	100.46
Value of the 4	400					$\frac{4}{100}$			

3 Complete the table below.

	Number in words	Number in figures
a	Three hundred and twenty-one	
b		732
c	Four thousand one hundred and twenty-six	
d		1662
e	Two thousand five hundred and eighty	
f	Two thousand five hundred and eight	
g		107
h		1090
i	Twenty-two point six	
j		71.45

4 **a** Write down the amount of money in each of the piles below.

_____ _____ _____ _____

b Put a circle around the largest amount. Put a square around the smallest amount.

Exercise 8B Multiplying and dividing by powers of 10

This exercise will give you practice in

○ multiplying and dividing positive integers by 10, 100 and 1000

 1 Complete each of the multiplication grids below.

×	10	100	1000
18			
540			
207			
98			

×	10	100	1000
73			
34			
150			
4603			

×	10	100	1000
	50		
31			
		8400	
			73 000

×	10	100	1000
83			
	2740		
		500	
			8000

2 Write down the answer to each of the following.

a 100 ÷ 10 = _____ **b** 4700 ÷ 10 = _____ **c** 650 ÷ 10 = _____

d 500 ÷ 100 = _____ **e** 2700 ÷ 100 = _____ **f** 21 500 ÷ 100 = _____

g 56 000 ÷ 1000 = _____ **h** 70 000 ÷ 1000 = _____ **i** 8000 ÷ 1000 = _____

3 Use the place value table to complete the sentences below.

T.Th	Th	H	T	U

a The effect of multiplying a whole number by 10 is that all the digits move one place to the left and the empty place is filled with a zero.

For example, 84 × 10 = _____.

b The effect of multiplying a whole number by 100 is that all the digits move two places to the left and the empty places are filled with zeros. For example,

763 × 100 = _____.

c The effect of multiplying a whole number by _____ is that all the digits move three places to the left and the empty places are filled with zeros. For example,

25 × 1000 = _____.

Exercise 8C Rounding

This exercise will give you practice in
- rounding positive whole numbers to the nearest 10, 100 and 1000

1 Round each of these numbers to the nearest multiple of 10.

Number	84	79	26	71	25	95	127	163	185	387	605	495
Number to the nearest 10												

2 Round each of these numbers to the nearest multiple of 100.

Number	264	381	167	923	850	95	649	198	450	550	1297	4312
Number to the nearest 100												

3 Round each of these numbers to the nearest multiple of 1000.

Number	1245	7639	4143	2754	1934	9499
Number to the nearest 1000						

Number	9050	3333	912	14 968	21 694	291 432
Number to the nearest 1000						

4 What is the volume of the liquid in each measuring cylinder to the nearest 10 ml?

a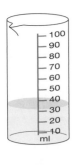

b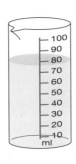

c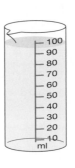

d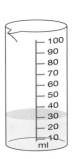

Exercise 8D Multiplying whole numbers

This exercise will give you practice in

- revising multiplication facts to 10 × 10
- completing TU × U and TU × TU multiplications using grid and column methods
- using a calculator for multiplications involving larger numbers

1 Fill in the boxes to complete the multiplication table below.

2 Write down the answers to each of the following.

a   3 × 8 _____

b   6 × 5 _____

c   2 × 9 _____

d   4 × 6 _____

e   5 × 7 _____

f   9 × 8 _____

g   6 × 4 _____

h   7 × 6 _____

i   9 × 5 _____

j   8 × 7 _____

k   6 × 6 _____

l   4 × 9 _____

m 9 × 4 _____

×	1	2	3	4	5	6	7	8	9	10
1	1		3	4			7		9	10
2	2	4	6		10		14	16		
3	3			12	15		21		27	30
4		8	12		20	24		32		40
5	5	10		20		30			45	
6	6		18			36	42			60
7		14		28	35		49	56	63	
8	8	16			40	48		64		80
9		18	27		45		63	72		90
10	10			40		60			90	

3 Fill in each of these grids and use them to work out the calculation underneath.

a

×	20	1
7		

21 × 7 = ☐ + ☐

= ☐

b

×	30	4
5		

34 × 5 = ☐ + ☐

= ☐

c

×	20	2
7		

22 × 7 = ☐ + ☐

= ☐

d

×	40	5
9		

45 × 9 = ☐ + ☐

= ☐

e

×	20	5
8		

25 × 8 = ☐ + ☐

= ☐

f

×	10	7
6		

17 × 6 = ☐ + ☐

= ☐

4 Use the grid method to work out each of the following calculations.

a

×		

16 × 4 = ☐ + ☐

= ☐

b

×		

23 × 8 = ☐ + ☐

= ☐

c

×		

41 × 7 = ☐ + ☐

= ☐

d

×		

18 × 5 = ☐ + ☐

= ☐

e

×		

63 × 4 = ☐ + ☐

= ☐

f

×		

32 × 9 = ☐ + ☐

= ☐

5 Use any method to work out each of the following multiplications.

a 21 × 3 ☐

b 16 × 5 ☐

c 12 × 6 ☐

d 14 × 4

e 21 × 13

f 12 × 43

6 Use a calculator to work out each of the following.

a 27 × 43 _____

b 82 × 49 _____

c 35 × 45 _____

d 73 × 32 _____

e 18 × 96 _____

f 176 × 41 _____

g 54 × 57 _____

h 265 × 190 _____

Exercise 8E Dividing whole numbers

This exercise will give you practice in
- learning and revising division facts

1 Write down the answer to each of the following divisions.

a 12 ÷ 3 _____

b 16 ÷ 4 _____

c 20 ÷ 5 _____

d 30 ÷ 2 _____

e 15 ÷ 3 _____

f 90 ÷ 10 _____

g 27 ÷ 9 _____

h 35 ÷ 5 _____

i 49 ÷ 7 _____

j 60 ÷ 6 _____

k 63 ÷ 9 _____

2 Complete each of the following divisions. You can copy these questions on to a separate sheet of paper if you need more space.

a 2)3 6

b 4)4 8

c 3)4 2

d 5)7 5

e 3)4 5

f 5)9 5

g 6)7 2

h 8)9 6

i 7)8 4

3 Use a calculator to work out each of the following.

a 84 ÷ 14 _____

b 96 ÷ 16 _____

c 48 ÷ 12 _____

d 99 ÷ 11 _____

e 90 ÷ 18 _____

f 52 ÷ 13 _____

g 87 ÷ 29 _____

h 85 ÷ 17 _____

i 324 ÷ 27 _____

Exercise 8F Multiplying and dividing decimals by powers of 10

This exercise will give you practice in
○ multiplying and dividing decimals by 10, 100 and 1000

1 Write down the answer to each of the following.

a 3.4 × 10 _____   **b** 8.3 × 10 _____   **c** 3.15 × 10 _____

d 3.02 × 10 _____   **e** 0.6 × 10 _____   **f** 0.05 × 10 _____

g 76 ÷ 10 _____   **h** 57.4 ÷ 10 _____   **i** 3.16 ÷ 10 _____

j 31.4 ÷ 10 _____   **k** 1.2 ÷ 10 _____   **l** 0.37 ÷ 10 _____

2 Write down the answer to each of the following.

a 4.2 × 100 _____   **b** 8.31 × 100 _____   **c** 24.5 × 100 _____

d 0.57 × 100 _____   **e** 0.04 × 100 _____   **f** 0.875 × 100 _____

g 960 ÷ 100 _____   **h** 277 ÷ 100 _____   **i** 113 ÷ 100 _____

j 83.8 ÷ 100 _____   **k** 8900 ÷ 100 _____   **l** 6.4 ÷ 100 _____

3 Write down the answer to each of the following.

a 15.199 × 1000 _____   **b** 9.732 × 1000 _____   **c** 23.52 × 1000 _____

d 10.2 × 1000 _____   **e** 0.491 × 1000 _____   **f** 0.042 × 1000 _____

g 8314 ÷ 1000 _____   **h** 2165 ÷ 1000 _____   **i** 17 563 ÷ 1000 _____

j 890 ÷ 1000 _____   **k** 75 ÷ 1000 _____   **l** 107 ÷ 1000 _____

4 Complete each of the multiplication grids below.

×	10	100	1000
3.2			
5.6			
1.07			
9.18			

×	10	100	1000
41.2			
3.41			
0.066			
7.32			

×	10	100	1000
0.025	0.25		
3.1			
		84	
			50.39

5 Complete the sentences below.

a The effect of multiplying a decimal by 10 is to move the digits one place to the left. For example, $3.49 \times 10 = 34.9$ and $2.7 \times 10 = $ _____ .

b The effect of dividing a decimal by 100 is to move the digits _____ places to the right. For example, $760 \div 100 = 7.6$ and $810 \div 100 = $ _____ .

c The effect of multiplying a decimal by _____ is to move the digits three places to the left. For example, $2.5 \times 1000 = 2500$ and $1.3 \times 1000 = $ _____ .

Exercise 8G Rounding decimals

This exercise will give you practice in
  ◦ rounding decimals to the nearest whole number

1 Round off each of these numbers to the nearest whole number.

a 6.9 _____   b 8.2 _____   c 11.6 _____

d 19.5 _____   e 2.3 _____   f 3.08 _____

g 5.14 _____   h 9.09 _____   i 6.75 _____

2 Complete the table by rounding each of the numbers to the nearest whole number.

Number	8.4	3.21	2.06	11.68	15.51	17.49	127.3	187.5	2045.43	1999.9	99.9	849.99
Nearest whole number												

Exercise 8H Adding and subtracting whole numbers

This exercise will give you practice in
○ adding and subtracting whole numbers

1 Work out each of the following additions.

a 3 + 7 _____   **b** 9 + 2 _____   **c** 8 + 5 _____

d 5 + 7 _____   **e** 9 + 6 _____   **f** 12 + 4 _____

g 22 + 8 _____   **h** 41 + 11 _____   **i** 24 + 15 _____

j 70 + 18 _____   **k** 15 + 22 _____   **l** 18 + 51 _____

2 Use any method to work out each of the following additions.

a 35 + 46   **b** 62 + 38   **c** 27 + 56

d 46 + 55   **e** 178 + 45   **f** 392 + 449

3 Fill in the missing numbers in each of the following additions.

a ☐ + 8 = 10   **b** 9 + ☐ = 12   **c** 15 + ☐☐ = 29

d ☐☐ + 42 = 68   **e** 3☐ + 17 = ☐8   **f** ☐5 + 6☐ = 88

4 Work out each of the following subtractions.

a 9 – 7 _____

b 8 – 5 _____

c 10 – 3 _____

d 12 – 4 _____

e 15 – 8 _____

f 17 – 6 _____

g 31 – 6 _____

h 24 – 15 _____

i 60 – 12 _____

5 Use any method to work out each of the following subtractions.

a 46 – 35

b 67 – 33

c 53 – 25

d 76 – 56

e 91 – 38

f 191 – 27

6 Fill in the missing numbers in each of the following subtractions.

a
```
    2  5
 -  1  □
 _____
    □  4
```

b
```
    8  6
 -  □  □
 _____
    3  5
```

c
```
    □  5
 -  1  9
 _____
    4  6
```

d
```
    3  1
 -  □  2
 _____
    1  □
```

e
```
    □  □
 -  4  3
 _____
    3  6
```

f
```
    □  □
 -  2  3
 _____
    1  7
```

7 Use a number line to work out each of the following. Use a separate sheet of paper if you need more space.

a 346 + 231 _____

b 847 + 267 _____

c 534 + 279 _____

d 353 – 169 _____

e 863 – 315 _____

f 891 – 620 _____

Exercise 81   Adding and subtracting decimals

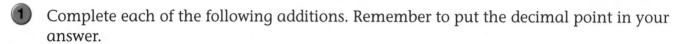

This exercise will give you practice in

○ adding and subtracting decimals

1 Complete each of the following additions. Remember to put the decimal point in your answer.

a	2.1	b	6.2	c	7.3
	+ 3.4		+ 1.7		+ 2.3

d	8.3	e	3.5	f	6.8
	+ 4.5		+ 4.2		+ 2.4

g	7.4	h	5.6	i	6.4
	+ 1.7		+ 8.5		+ 4.9

2 Complete each of the following subtractions. Remember to put the decimal point in your answer.

a	6.5	b	9.1	c	4.7
	– 3.4		– 6.0		– 3.2

d	8.6	e	1.9	f	8.1
	− 5.5		− 0.7		− 1.6

g	8.3	h	7.6	i	4.5
	− 4.9		− 2.8		− 3.6

3 Work out each of the following in the space below. Remember to put the decimal point in your answer.

a 4.1 + 2.5 + 3.2

b 4.5 − 1.2 − 2.3

c 7.3 − 3.7 − 2.5

d 6.7 + 3 − 5.7

CHAPTER 9 Geometry and measures 3

Exercise 9A Reflections and symmetry

This exercise will give you practice in
- reflecting 2-D shapes in mirror lines
- drawing lines of symmetry

1. Draw a line of symmetry onto each of the following diagrams.

2. Draw all of the lines of symmetry onto the following letters.

3. Draw the lines of symmetry onto each of the following diagrams.

4. For each of the following shapes, write down the name and the number of lines of symmetry.

a   b   c   d   e

_____ _____ _____ _____ _____

_____ _____ _____ _____ _____

Exercise 9B   Rotations

This exercise will give you practice in

○ rotating a 2-D shape about a given point

① Rotate each of the following flags about the point marked × through the angle indicated.

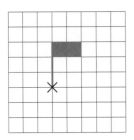 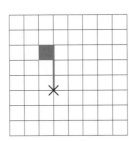 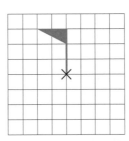 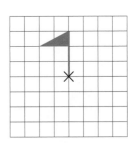

90° clockwise   90° clockwise   90° clockwise   90° clockwise

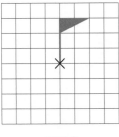 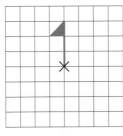 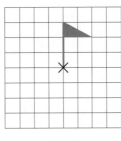 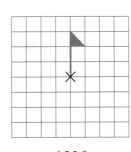

180°   180°   180°   180°

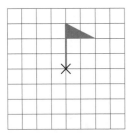 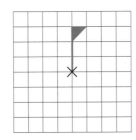 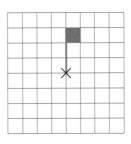 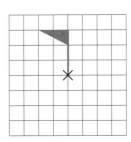

90° anticlockwise   90° anticlockwise   90° anticlockwise   90° anticlockwise

Exercise 9C   Translations

This exercise will give you practice in

○ translating (moving) a 2-D shape

1 Translate (move) each of the following shapes as described.

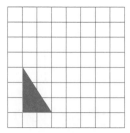

3 squares right

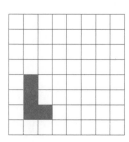

3 squares right
1 square up

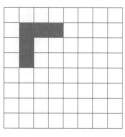

3 squares right
2 squares down

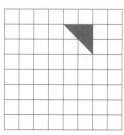

1 square left
4 squares down

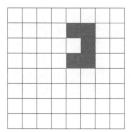

2 squares left
3 squares down

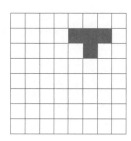

4 squares left
3 squares down

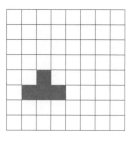

2 squares right
4 squares up

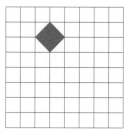

2 squares right
3 squares down

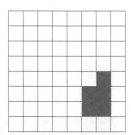

4 squares left
2 squares up

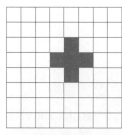

3 squares left
1 square down

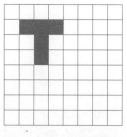

3 squares right
3 squares down

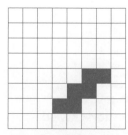

2 squares left
3 squares up

Exercise 10A Solving equations

This exercise will give you practice in

- solving equations

1 Fill in the weighing scales to solve each equation.
The first one has been done for you.

a $x + 2 = 5$

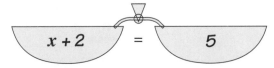

Subtract 2 from both sides

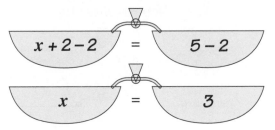

b $x + 5 = 9$

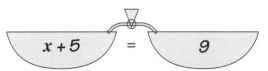

Subtract 5 from both sides

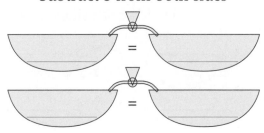

c $x + 10 = 15$

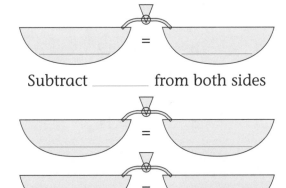

Subtract _____ from both sides

d $x - 2 = 6$

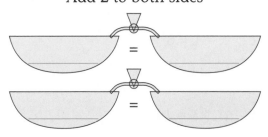

Add 2 to both sides

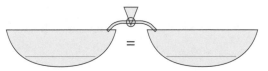

e $x - 6 = 10$

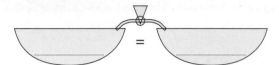

Add 6 to both sides

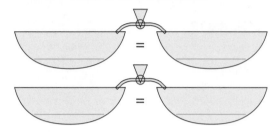

f $x - 3 = 12$

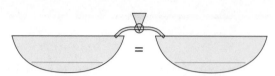

Add _____ to both sides

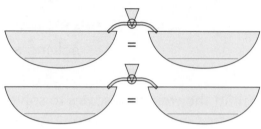

g $2x = 8$

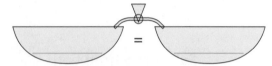

Divide both sides by 2

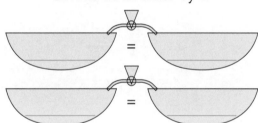

h $5x = 15$

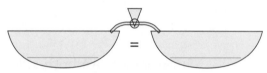

Divide both sides by _____

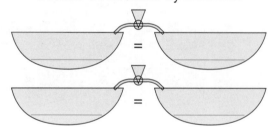

2   Solve each equation by filling in the value of x.

a $x + 4 = 10$

$x = $ _____

b $x + 9 = 12$

$x = $ _____

c $x - 4 = 8$

$x = $ _____

d $x - 7 = 11$

$x = $ _____

e $2x = 14$

$x = $ _____

f $3x = 18$

$x = $ _____

g $5x = 20$

$x = $ _____

h $2x + 1 = 7$

$2x = $ _____

$x = $ _____

Exercise 10B **Algebraic expressions**

This exercise will give you practice in
- writing out expressions using algebra
- using letters for numbers

1 Match each of the word statements on the left to an expression on the right. The letter n stands for a number. The first one has been done for you.

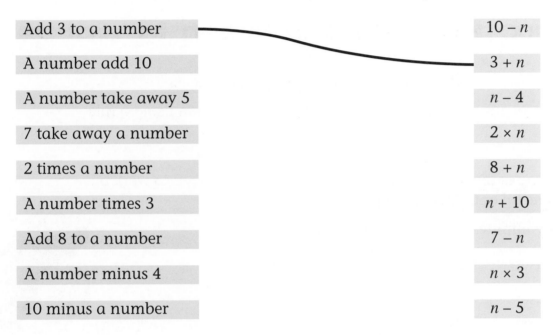

Add 3 to a number	$10 - n$
A number add 10	$3 + n$
A number take away 5	$n - 4$
7 take away a number	$2 \times n$
2 times a number	$8 + n$
A number times 3	$n + 10$
Add 8 to a number	$7 - n$
A number minus 4	$n \times 3$
10 minus a number	$n - 5$

2 Write each of these expressions as word statements.

a $n + 5$ _____

b $n \times 7$ _____

c $n - 2$ _____

d $n \div 3$ _____

e $4 + n$ _____

f $5 - n$ _____

g $8 \times n$ _____

h $10 \div n$ _____

3 Write down the value of each expression for the value of n given.

a $n = 4$ $n + 1 =$ _____ $n + 3 =$ _____ $n + 5 =$ _____

b $n = 10$ $n - 1 =$ _____ $n - 3 =$ _____ $n - 5 =$ _____

c $n = 3$ $n \times 1 =$ _____ $n \times 3 =$ _____ $n \times 5 =$ _____

d $n = 8$ $n \div 1 =$ _____ $n \div 2 =$ _____ $n \div 4 =$ _____

(4) Write down the value of each expression for the value of n given.

a $n = 3$ $n \times 2 =$ _____ $2 \times n =$ _____ $2n =$ _____

b $n = 10$ $n \times 3 =$ _____ $3 \times n =$ _____ $3n =$ _____

c $n = 3$ $n \times 4 =$ _____ $4 \times n =$ _____ $4n =$ _____

Exercise 10C Formulae written in words

This exercise will give you practice in

○ calculating the answer to a problem using a rule

(1) A postman uses the rule **time taken = number of houses × 2** to work out how long he takes to deliver the post.

How many minutes does it take him to deliver to

a 30 houses? _____

b 50 houses? _____

c 200 houses? _____

(2) A fairground ride charges £3 per person. The rule to work out how much money the fairground ride takes is **total money taken = number of people × £3**.

How much money does the fairground ride take if there are

a 10 people on the ride? _____

b 20 people on the ride? _____

c 50 people on the ride? _____

(3) Sarah charges £2.50 to wash one car. The rule to work out the money she makes is **money made = number of cars washed × £2.50**.

On the next page, match up the number of cars she washed to the amount of money she made.

Exercise 10D Substituting into formulae

This exercise will give you practice in

- using a formula or rule

1 Trevor is 3 years older than Belinda. The formula for working out Trevor's age is

$T = B + 3$ where T = Trevor's age

                        B = Belinda's age

Use the formula to work out Trevor's age when Belinda's age is

a 20 years _____

b 49 years _____

c 72 years _____

2 A driving instructor uses this formula to work out how long he works.

$h = 5d$ where h = the total number of hours he works

                        d = the number of days he works

Use the formula to work out the number of hours he works in

a 3 days _____

b 7 days _____

c 20 days _____

3 Work out the value of H when $T = 10$ using the formula $H = T - 7$.

$H =$ _____ $- 7$

$H =$ _____

4 Work out the value of y when $x = 5$ using the formula $y = x + 9$.

$y =$ _____ $+ 9$

$y =$ _____

5 Work out the value of P when $C = 8$ using the formula $P = C \times 5$.

$P =$ _____ $\times 5$

$P =$ _____

6 Work out the value of A when $l = 8$ and $w = 5$ using the formula
$A = l \times w$

$A =$ _____ $\times$ _____

$A =$ _____

Exercise 11A Information from charts

1 The charts below show the distances, in miles, between certain cities in the UK.

Cardiff			
150	London		
398	412	Edinburgh	
246	208	191	York

Complete the sentences.

a   The distance from Cardiff to London is _____ miles.

b   The distance from London to York is _____ miles.

c   The distance from Edinburgh to Cardiff is _____ miles.

d   The distance from _____ to _____ is 246 miles.

e   The distance from _____ to _____ is 191 miles.

f   The distance from _____ to _____ is 412 miles.

2 The table shows part of a bus timetable from Rotherham to Ravenfield.

Rotherham	0815	0908
Wickersley	0838	0931
Flanderwell	0842	0935
Woodlaithes	0849	0942
Ravenfield	0854	0947

Complete the sentences.

a   The buses leave Rotherham at 0815 and _____

b   The 0815 bus from Rotherham is due at Wickersley at _____

c   The 0908 bus from Rotherham is due at Wickersley at _____

d   The 0908 bus from Rotherham is due at Ravenfield at _____

e   From Flanderwell to Woodlaithes it takes _____ minutes.

f   From Rotherham to Ravenfield it takes _____ minutes.

(3) The table shows the favourite pastimes of a group of pupils.

	Watch TV	Sport	Computer	Reading
Boys	4	8	6	2
Girls	5	7	3	5

a   How many pupils are in the group? _____

b   How many boys chose Sport? _____

c   How many girls chose Computer or Reading? _____

d   How many pupils chose Watch TV? _____

e   Which pastime was the most popular? _____

f   Which pastime was the least popular? _____

(4) The table shows the times of some TV programmes.

11.00	Saturday Cooking
11.45	Football Preview
12.00	News
12.20	Weather
12.30	Cartoons
12.50	The Film Show
3.00 – 3.10	Around the Grounds

a   How long is Saturday Cooking? _____ minutes

b   What time does Cartoons start? _____

c   What time does the Weather end? _____

d   Which programme starts at quarter to twelve? _____

e   Which programme ends at twenty past twelve? _____

f   How long does The Film Show last? _____

Exercise 11B Bar-line graphs

This exercise will give you practice in

○ drawing bar-line graphs

1 For each table draw a bar-line graph.

a

Favourite food	Tally	Frequency
Chips	JHT	
Salad	JHT JHT JHT II	
Burger	JHT JHT	
Beans	JHT III	

b

Favourite colour	Tally	Frequency
Blue	II	
Red	JHT JHT	
Yellow	JHT JHT JHT IIII	
Green	JHT I	

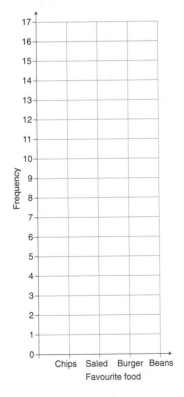

a

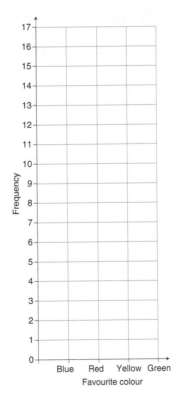

b

2 A dice is rolled 30 times. The scores are shown in the table.

Score	Frequency
1	5
2	2
3	7
4	4
5	9
6	3

a Draw a bar-line graph on the grid to show the results.

b Do you think the dice is fair? Explain your answer.

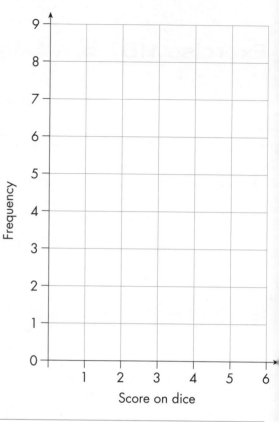

3 Katie asked her friends what their favourite day of the week is. The results are shown in the table.

Favourite day	Frequency
Monday	0
Tuesday	3
Wednesday	5
Thursday	4
Friday	7
Saturday	9
Sunday	6

a Draw a bar-line graph on the grid to show the results.

b Which day is the most popular?

c How many people did Katie ask?

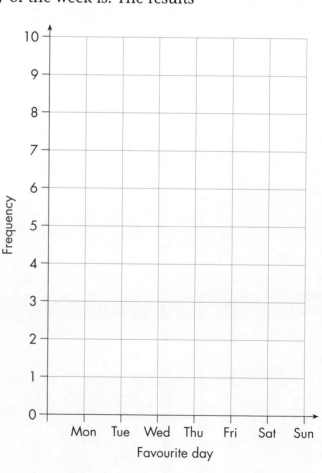

Exercise 11C Pie charts

This exercise will give you practice in

○ drawing 10 sector pie charts

1 Complete each of the following tables and draw a pie chart to show the data. Remember to put labels on your pie charts.

a

Favourite colour	Number of students	Number of sectors on pie chart
Red	4	4
Blue	1	
Yellow	3	
Green	2	
	Total = 10	**Total = 10**

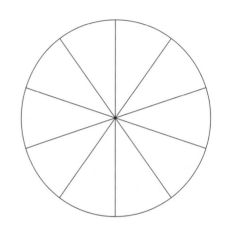

b

Favourite music	Number of students	Number of sectors on pie chart
Rock	6	3
Classical	2	
Rap	8	
Hip hop	4	
	Total = 20	**Total = 10**

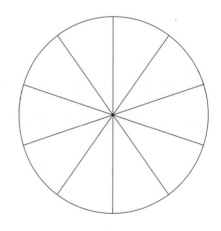

c

Pets	Number of pets	Number of sectors on pie chart
Dog	20	4
Cat	15	
Fish	5	
Other	10	
	Total = 50	**Total = 10**

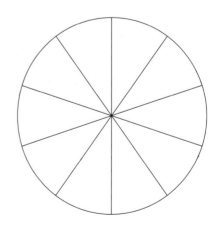

d

Arrival of buses	Frequency	Number of sectors on pie chart
Early	10%	1
On time	55%	
Late	35%	
	Total = 100%	**Total = 10**

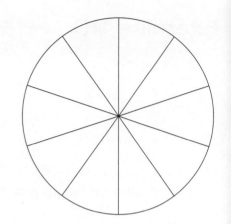

Exercise 12A Order of operations

This exercise will give you practice in

○ using a calculator including using brackets and the memory

1 Without using a calculator, complete the following. Remember to work out any multiplications and divisions before additions or subtractions.

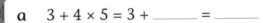

a $3 + 4 \times 5 = 3 +$ _____ = _____

b $3 \times 4 + 5 =$ _____ $+ 5 =$ _____

c $4 \div 2 + 1 =$ _____ $+ 1 =$ _____

d $5 + 4 \div 2 = 5 +$ _____ = _____

2 Without using a calculator, complete the following. Remember to work out any brackets first.

a $6 + (4 \times 3) = 6 +$ _____ = _____

b $4 + (3 \times 6) = 4 +$ _____ = _____

c $(6 + 4) \times 3 =$ _____ $\times 3 =$ _____

d $(8 + 1) + (8 \div 4) =$ _____ $+$ _____ = _____

3 Use a calculator to work out each of the following.

a $3.2 \times 4 + 7.3$ _____

b $8.1 \times 3.5 - 7.9$ _____

c $3.4 + (9.8 \times 7.3)$ _____

d $2.7 + (13.5 \div 0.5)$ _____

e $(3.1 + 19.7) \div (8.3 - 6.3)$ _____

f $(67.4 + 22.6) \div (8.1 \div 0.27)$ _____

g $\dfrac{(4.7 \times 2.1)}{(2.3 + 7.7)}$ _____

h $\dfrac{(98.6 \times 2.04)}{(27.3 - 7.3)}$ _____

4 Use a calculator to work out each of the following. Use the memory button to work out the multiplication or division before the addition or subtraction.

a $21 + 35 \times 62$ _____

b $83 + 47 \times 98$ _____

c $6.7 - 2.2 \times 3.4$ _____

d $403 - 45 \times 7$ _____

e $1000 - 38 \times 5$ _____

f $250 + 98 \div 7$ _____

g $8.9 + 183 \div 30$ _____

h $32 \times 42 + 27 \times 21$ _____

5 Join each of the following questions to the correct answer using a straight line. Remember to work out the multiplication or division before the addition or subtraction.

Questions	Answers
84 + 27 × 51	2301
63 + 42 × 31	6
76 + 25 × 89	1461
35 + 51 ÷ 17	59
63 – 124 ÷ 31	1365
286 – 196 ÷ 0.7	38

Exercise 12B Multiplication facts

This exercise will give you practice in
- using known multiplication facts

1 Calculate each of the following.

a	3 × 10 _____	b	30 × 10 _____	c	30 × 100 _____
d	40 × 20 _____	e	30 × 40 _____	f	20 × 20 _____
g	20 × 300 _____	h	50 × 30 _____	i	50 × 60 _____

2 Fill in the missing number in each of the following calculations.

a   5 × 30 = _____

b   4 × _____ = 100

c   6 × 50 = _____

d   100 × _____ = 700

e   20 × 30 = _____

f   40 × _____ = 800

3 Fill in the missing numbers in each of the following calculations.

a   _____ × _____ = 25

b   _____ × _____ = 30

c   _____ × _____ = 15

d   _____ × _____ = 18

e   _____ ÷ _____ = 10

f   _____ ÷ _____ = 15

g   _____ ÷ _____ = 8

h   _____ ÷ _____ = 12

4 **a** What is nine multiplied by five? _____

b What is seven multiplied by four? _____

c What is seven hundred and twenty divided by ten? _____

d What is six hundred and forty-one divided by one hundred? _____

e A pen costs £1.99. What do 2 pens cost? _____

f A pen costs £1.99.

    i How many pens can I buy for £10? _____

    ii How much change will I receive? _____

g What is two thousand divided by two hundred? _____

h What is eight point six multiplied by one hundred? _____

i What is thirty-six divided by six? _____

Exercise 12C Multiplying and dividing with large numbers

This exercise will give you practice in

○ multiplying and dividing using large numbers

1 Fill in each of these grids and use them to work out the calculation underneath.

a

×	20	3	
2			

23 × 2 = _____

b

×	30	4	
5			

34 × 5 = _____

c

×	3
60	
1	

3 × 61 = _____

d

×	5
20	
4	

5 × 24 = _____

e

×	200	30	1	
7				

231 × 7 = _____

f

×	6
200	
40	
1	

6 × 241 = _____

g

×	4
500	
10	
3	

4 × 513 = _____

h

×	20	3
100		
40		
2		

23 × 142 = _____

i

×	40	1
200		
50		
1		

41 × 251 = _____

j

×	300	10	2
20			
4			

312 × 24 = _____

2 A kilogram of apples costs 91p. How much do 3 kilograms cost? _____

3 15 cars pass my house every minute. How many cars will pass my house in 5 minutes? _____

4 Use any division method to work out the following calculations.

a 84 ÷ 6 = _____   b 54 ÷ 3 = _____

c 64 ÷ 4 = _____   d 144 ÷ 3 = _____

e 72 ÷ 4 = _____   f 85 ÷ 5 = _____

5 Five lorries carry 200 tonnes of pipes. If they all carry the same amount, how much does one lorry carry? _____

6 720 people use a cash machine in 6 hours.

    a How many people would use the cash machine in 1 hour? _____

    b How many people would use the cash machine in 1 minute? _____

Exercise 12D Multiplying and dividing decimals by whole numbers

This exercise will give you practice in

○ multiplying and dividing decimals by whole numbers

1 Complete each of the following multiplications. Remember to put the decimal point in your answer.

a	b	c
2.3 × 2	3.1 × 3	1.4 × 2

d	e	f
3.5 × 4	1.8 × 3	1.1 × 9

g	h	i
3.4 × 6	1.7 × 5	5.36 × 2

2 Complete each of the following divisions. Remember to put the decimal point in your answer.

  a 2)6.4   **b** 5)3.5   **c** 4)4.8

  d 7)7.7   **e** 3)12.3   **f** 4)5.6

  g 3)4.2   **h** 3)6.12   **i** 4)7.24

Exercise 13A **Plotting coordinates**

This exercise will give you practice in

○ plotting coordinates on graph paper

1 Plot each of the following sets of coordinates on the grid. Join the points with straight lines, in order. Try to guess what you are drawing.

a (3, 10), (4, 10), (5, 9), (6, 9), (7, 10), (8, 10), (10, 8), (9, 7), (8, 8), (8, 3), (3, 3), (3, 8), (2, 7), (1, 8), (3, 10)

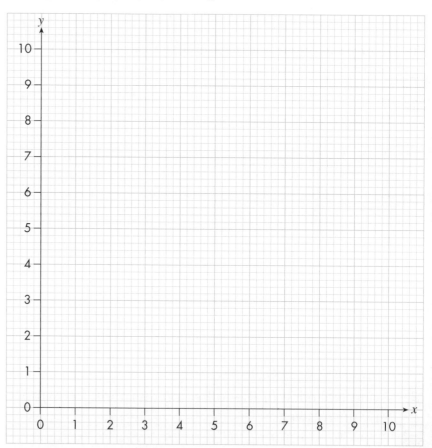

b (4, 7), (3, 7), (0, 9), (0, 3),
   (3, 5), (4, 5), (4, 4), (6, 4),
   (6, 5), (7, 5), (10, 3), (10, 9),
   (7, 7), (6, 7), (6, 5), (6, 8),
   (4, 8), (4, 5)

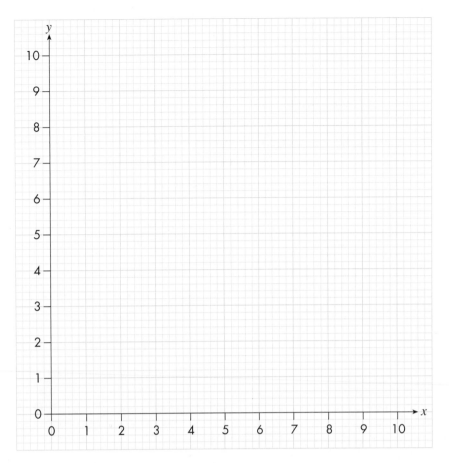

c (3, 3), (2, 4), (2, 6), (3, 7),
   (3, 8), (4, 9), (5, 8), (5, 7),
   (4, 6), (4, 5), (5, 5), (5, 6),
   (4, 6), (5, 7), (6, 7), (7, 6),
   (7, 5), (6, 5), (6, 6), (7, 6),
   (6, 7), (6, 8), (7, 9), (8, 8),
   (8, 7), (9, 6), (9, 4), (8, 3),
   (7, 4), (8, 4), (7, 4), (8, 5),
   (6, 3), (5, 3), (3, 5), (4, 4),
   (3, 4), (4, 4), (3, 3), (4, 2),
   (7, 2), (8, 3)

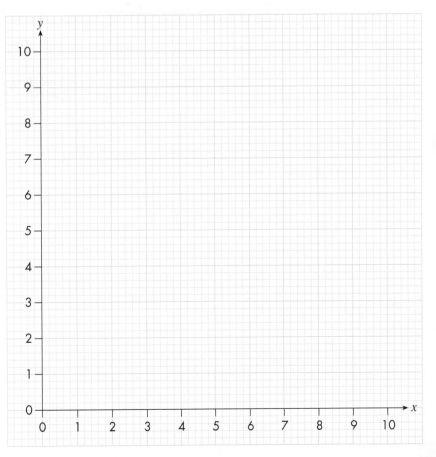

d (5, 9), (4, 10), (3, 10), (1, 8),
(1, 5), (4, 2), (6, 2), (6, 3),
(5, 4), (6, 3), (7, 3), (8, 4),
(8, 5), (6, 5), (9, 5), (10, 6),
(7, 6), (6.5, 6.5), (7, 6),
(8, 6), (9, 7), (9, 8), (8, 9),
(7, 9), (6.5, 8.5), (7, 8),
(7, 7), (6, 6), (5, 6), (4, 7),
(4, 8), (5, 9), (6, 9), (6.5, 8.5)

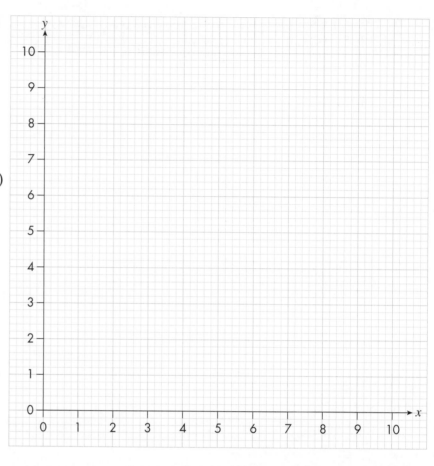

Exercise 13B Generating coordinates

This exercise will give you practice in

- generating coordinates using a rule or formula

① Complete each of the following tables by generating the
y-coordinates. Use the table to plot the coordinates on the grid.

a

x	0	1	2	3	4
$y = x + 3$					

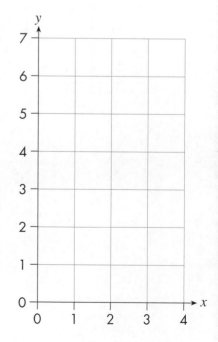

b

x	0	1	2	3	4
$y = x - 1$					

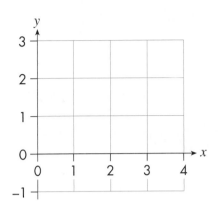

c

x	3	2	1	0	−1	−2
$y = 2x$						

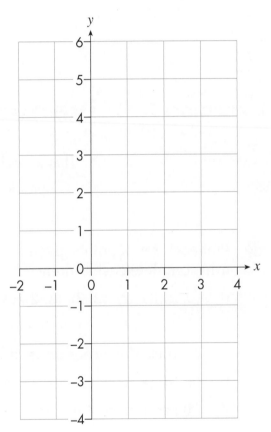

d

x	0	1	2	3	4
$y = 4 - x$					

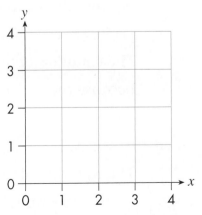

e

x	–3	–2	–1	0	1	2	3
$y = x + 2$							

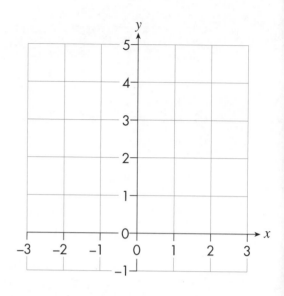

Exercise 13C Naming and drawing graphs

This exercise will give you practice in

○ naming graphs through two or more points

① Plot each set of points given on the grid. Join the points with a ruled line and complete each sentence.

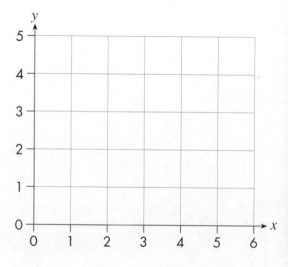

a (0, 2), (1, 2), (2, 2), (3, 2), (4, 2), (5, 2), (6, 2)

The equation of the line is $y =$ _____

because the y-coordinate is always _____ .

b (4, 0), (4, 1), (4, 2), (4, 3), (4, 4), (4, 5)

The equation of the line is $x =$ _____

because the x-coordinate is always _____ .

c (1, 0), (1, 1), (1, 2), (1, 3), (1, 4), (1, 5)

The equation of the line is _____ = _____

because the _____-coordinate is always

_____ .

d (0, 3), (1, 3), (2, 3), (3, 3), (4, 3), (5, 3), (6, 3)

The equation of the line is _____ = _____ because the

_____-coordinate is always _____ .

2 Draw each of the following graphs on the grid and label them.

a $x = 2$

b $x = 5$

c $y = 4$

d $y = 6$

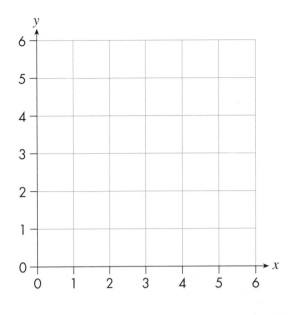

3 Label each of the lines drawn on the grid below.

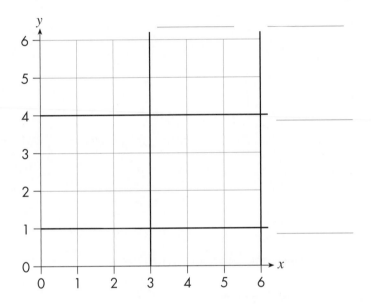

Exercise 13D Naming and drawing sloping lines

This exercise will give you practice in

- naming and drawing sloping lines

1 Plot the following points on the grid. Join the points with a ruled line and complete each sentence.

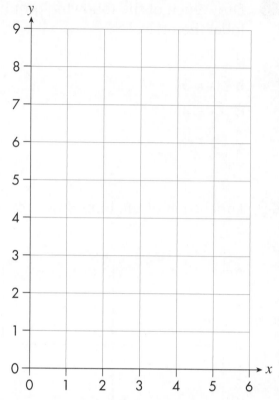

a (0, 0), (1, 1), (2, 2), (3, 3), (4, 4), (5, 5), (6, 6)

The equation of the line is $y = x$ because the y-coordinate is always the same as the

_____ -coordinate.

b (0, 1), (1, 2), (2, 3), (3, 4), (4, 5), (5, 6), (6, 7)

The equation of the line is $y = x + 1$ because the y-coordinate is always _____ more than the _____ -_____ .

c (1, 0), (2, 1), (3, 2), (4, 3), (5, 4), (6, 5)

The equation of the line is $y =$ _____

because the y-coordinate is always _____

less than the _____ -_____ .

d (0, 0), (1, 2), (2, 4), (3, 6), (4, 8)

The equation of the line is $y =$ _____ because the y-coordinate is always double or _____ times the _____ -_____ .

e (0, 0), (1, 3), (2, 6), (3, 9)

The equation of the line is $y =$ _____ because the y-coordinate is always _____ _____ the _____ -_____ .

f (0, 5), (1, 6), (2, 7), (3, 8), (4, 9)

The equation of the line is $y =$ _____ because the y-coordinate is always _____ more than the _____ -_____ .

Exercise 14A Solving problems using near doubles

This exercise will give you practice in

- calculating near doubles

1 Fill in the missing numbers below.

a $200 + 200 = \underline{\hspace{1cm}}$

$206 = 200 + \underline{\hspace{1cm}}$

$199 = 200 - \underline{\hspace{1cm}}$

$206 + 199 = 200 + \underline{\hspace{1cm}} + 200 - 1$

$= 400 + \underline{\hspace{1cm}}$

$= \underline{\hspace{1cm}}$

b $80 + 80 = \underline{\hspace{1cm}}$

$83 + 86 = 80 + \underline{\hspace{1cm}} + 80 + \underline{\hspace{1cm}}$

$= \underline{\hspace{1cm}} + \underline{\hspace{1cm}}$

$= \underline{\hspace{1cm}}$

c $140 + 140 = \underline{\hspace{1cm}}$

$143 + 139 = 140 + \underline{\hspace{1cm}} + 140 - \underline{\hspace{1cm}}$

$= \underline{\hspace{1cm}} + \underline{\hspace{1cm}}$

$= \underline{\hspace{1cm}}$

d $250 + 250 = \underline{\hspace{1cm}}$

$252 + 246 = 250 + \underline{\hspace{1cm}} + 250 - \underline{\hspace{1cm}}$

$= \underline{\hspace{1cm}} - \underline{\hspace{1cm}}$

$= \underline{\hspace{1cm}}$

2 Use the number line to work out the answers to each of the following.
The first one has been done for you.

a $106 + 112 = 218$

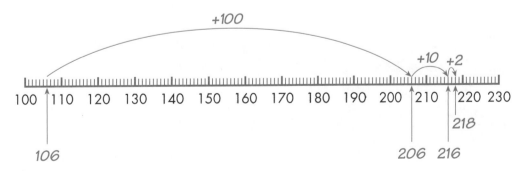

b   91 + 90 = _____

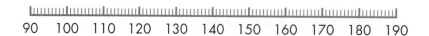

90   100   110   120   130   140   150   160   170   180   190

c   38 + 43 = _____

30   40   50   60   70   80   90

d   165 + 157 = _____

160   170   180   190   200   210   220   230   240   250   260   270   280   290   300   310   320   330

③   Work out the total cost of each of the following.

a

£ 4.99   +   £ 4.99

Total cost = _____

b

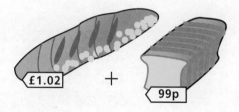

£1.02   +   99p

Total cost = _____

c

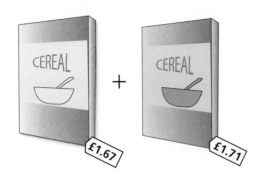

Total cost = _____

Exercise 14B Money problems

This exercise will give you practice in

- solving questions involving money

1. Calculate the total cost of each of the following shopping bills.

a

	Cost
Bread	£0.72
Soup	£0.45
Tea bags	£1.60
Total = _____	

b

	Cost
Fish	£2.43
Frozen chips	£1.69
Peas	£0.35
Total = _____	

c

	Cost
Trousers	£25.00
Shirt	£4.99
Tie	£9.50
Total = _____	

2 Complete the following table.

Price	Change from £5	Change from £10
£4.50	50p	£5.50
£4.99		
£3.20		
£2.99		
£1.80		
60p		
£3.79		

3 How many of each of the following items could you buy for £10?

a Tickets costing £3 each _____

b Oranges costing 49p each _____

c Cards costing £1.50 each _____

d Burgers costing £1.99 each _____

e Dolls costing £7.49 each _____

4 A DIY store sells nails by the kilogram. The following table shows the cost of different sized nails.

a Bob buys 1 kg of 40 mm nails and 1 kg of 100 mm nails. How much does he pay altogether?

_____

b Hareth bought 1 kg of nails and paid with a £2 coin. He got 57p change. What size nails did he buy?

_____

Size	Price per kilogram
25 mm	£2.10
40 mm	£1.50
50 mm	£1.43
65 mm	£1.36
75 mm	£1.32
100 mm	£1.30

5 Look at the fare table for a bus route shown on the right.

a How much is the fare from Barnsley to Penistone?

_____

b How much is the fare from Silkstone to Hoylandswaine?

_____

c Harriet pays £1.05. Between which two places is she travelling?

_____

Barnsley			
55p	Dodworth		
75p	45p	Silkstone	
£1.20	60p	35p	Hoylandswaine
£1.40	£1.05	65p	35p	Penistone

Exercise 14C Division problems

This exercise will give you practice in

○ interpreting answers to division problems

1 A minibus can carry up to 10 passengers.

a How many minibuses would be needed to carry 18 passengers? _____

b How many empty seats would there be? _____

2 50 people are queuing for a roller coaster. There are 24 seats on each ride.

How many rides are there before the last person in the queue can get on? _____

3 A teacher always uses four pins to put posters up on the wall. She has 30 pins.

a How many posters can she put up? _____

b How many pins will she have left over? _____

4 Betty has £100 to spend on books. Each books costs £11.

a How many books can Betty buy? _____

b How much money will she have left over? _____

5 A teacher has 50 sheets of plain paper to share out equally among 15 pupils.

    a Who is correct? Explain your answer.

_____

_____

    b How many sheets of paper will the teacher

       have left over? _____

We will each get 4 sheets of paper.

Jonathan

We will each get 3 sheets of paper.

Matthew

Exercise 14D Ratios and better value

This exercise will give you practice in

    ● using ratios and proportions

1 Write down the ratio of red : white for each of the following situations.

    a _____

    b _____

    c _____

    d _____   **e** _____   **f** _____

2 Draw a line to match up the equivalent ratios.

1 : 4   3 : 2   3 : 1   2 : 1

1 : 2   2 : 8   6 : 4   10 : 5

9 : 3   4 : 8

3 For each bag of red and black beads, write down the ratio in its simplest form.

a

Red : Black = _____ : _____

= _____ : _____

b

Red : Black = _____ : _____

= _____ : _____

c

Red : Black = _____ : _____

= _____ : _____

d

Red : Black = _____ : _____

= _____ : _____

4 Look at each of the following diagrams and work out which is the better value.

a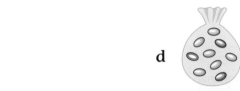

_____

b

£1.50   £4.80

_____

c

£1.25   £2.40

WATER   WATER

1 litre   2 litre

_____

d

£1.35 fish fingers 10   £2.75 fish fingers 20

_____

Exercise 14E Solving problems using ratios and proportions

This exercise will give you practice in

- solving problems using ratios and proportions

1 A painter makes pink paint by mixing red paint and white paint. Look at the pictures and number the mixtures from lightest to darkest.

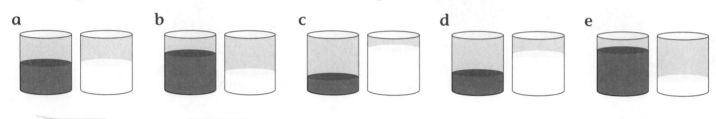

a   b   c   d   e

2 There are 30 students in a class. There are twice as many girls as boys.

How many girls are there? _____

3 There are 30 students in a class. Chris says that exactly $\frac{1}{4}$ are boys.

Explain how you know that Chris is not correct.

_____

_____

4 Tom shares 24 sweets with Jeff. Jeff only gets half as many as Tom.

How many sweets does Jeff get? _____

5 Mrs Rodley has seven rulers. She shares them out so that there is a ruler for every three students.

How many students are in the class? _____

6 Look at the recipe for making 12 Yorkshire Puddings.

Fill in the gaps in the table below.

> 400 g plain flour
> 2 eggs
> 1 pint of milk

	12 Yorkshire puddings	6 Yorkshire puddings	24 Yorkshire puddings	18 Yorkshire puddings
Plain flour	400 g		800 g	
Eggs	2	1		
Milk	1 pint			$1\frac{1}{2}$ pints

CHAPTER 15

Geometry and measures 4

Exercise 15A 3-D shapes

This exercise will give you practice in

- recognising 3-D shapes
- understanding the properties of 3D shapes

1 Complete the table below by putting the name of each shape next to the correct picture and filling in the number of faces, edges and vertices.

Square-based pyramid   Triangular prism   Cube   Sphere

Cuboid   Hemisphere   Tetrahedron

	Name	Faces	Edges	Vertices

2 **a** On the isometric grid on the next page, copy each of the shapes but make all of the lengths in your shape **twice** as long as the original.

b Shade the faces of your shapes using one colour as shown.

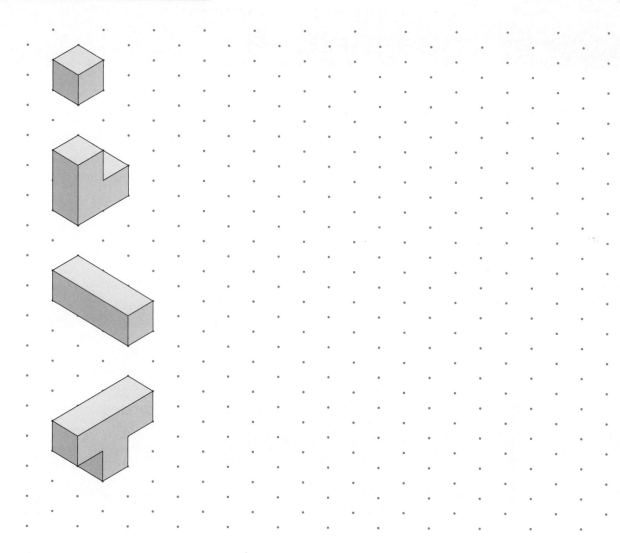

Exercise 15B Nets of 3-D shapes

This exercise will give you practice in

○ drawing nets of 3-D shapes

(1) Look at each of the following nets and write down the name of the
3-D shape that can be formed.

a   b   c   d

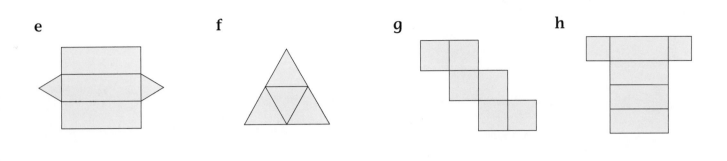

e   f   g   h

2 Draw the net of each of the following 3-D shapes on the centimetre-square
   grid below and on the next page.

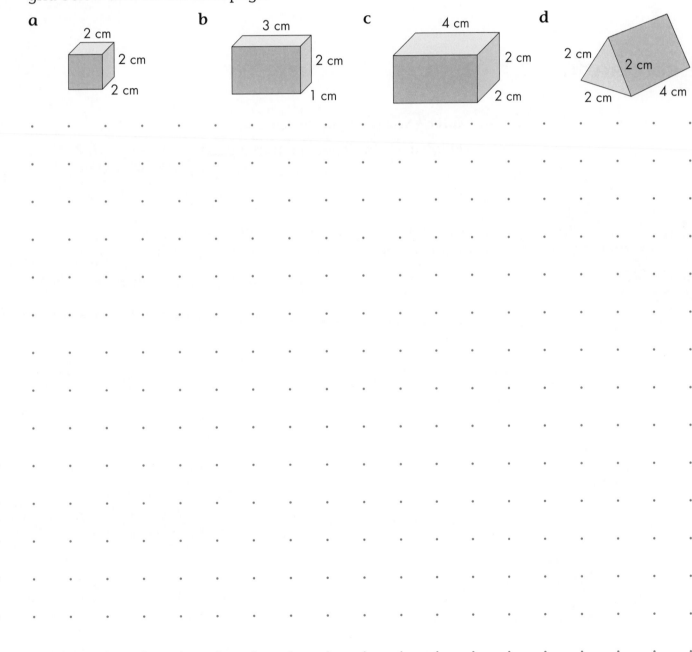

a   b   c   d

2 cm   3 cm   4 cm   2 cm
2 cm   2 cm   2 cm   2 cm
2 cm   1 cm   2 cm   2 cm   4 cm

Exercise 15C Drawing triangles

This exercise will give you practice in

- making accurate drawings of triangles

(1) Use a ruler and a protractor to make an accurate drawing of each of the following triangles. Measure and label all of the other angles and sides on your drawing.

a

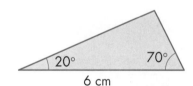

20° 70°
6 cm

b

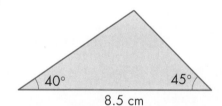

40° 45°
8.5 cm

c

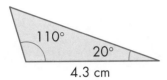

110°
20°
4.3 cm

d

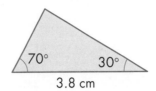

70°   30°
3.8 cm

2 Use a ruler and a protractor to make an accurate drawing of each of the following triangles. Measure and label all of the other angles and sides on your drawing.

a

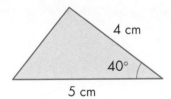

4 cm
40°
5 cm

b

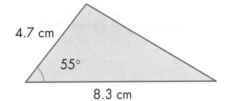

4.7 cm
55°
8.3 cm

c

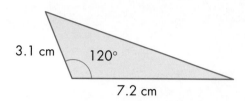

3.1 cm

120°

7.2 cm

d

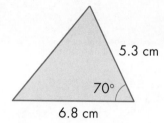

5.3 cm

70°

6.8 cm

Exercise 16A Frequency tables

This exercise will give you practice in
- collecting data into a grouped frequency table

1 Here are the scores of 20 pupils in a short test.

5	3	5	1	0	2	2	5	4	1
2	4	2	1	0	5	3	5	2	4

Using this data, complete the frequency table.

Score	Tally	Frequency
0		
1		
2		
3		
4		
5		

2 20 students are asked a question. They take the following lengths of time to answer (to the nearest minute).

2 min, 6 min, 10 min, 1 min, 3 min, 4 min, 4 min, 6 min, 8 min, 7 min, 6 min, 2 min, 9 min, 5 min, 5 min, 7 min, 1 min, 4 min, 5 min, 4 min

a Using this data, complete the grouped frequency table.

Time (minutes)	Tally	Frequency
1–2		
3–4		
5–6		
7–8		
9–10		

b Use your grouped frequency table to draw a bar chart on the axes provided.

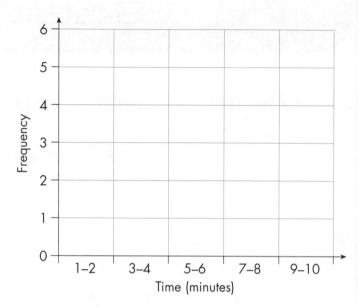

3 The height of 20 plants is measured. The heights are given below.

18 cm, 23 cm, 12 cm, 27 cm, 32 cm, 12 cm, 34 cm, 37 cm, 14 cm, 9 cm, 8 cm, 15 cm, 36 cm, 32 cm, 27 cm, 25 cm, 22 cm, 25 cm, 7 cm, 13 cm

a Using this data, complete the grouped frequency table.

Height (cm)	Tally	Frequency
1–10		
11–20		
21–30		
31–40		

b Use your grouped frequency table to draw a bar chart on the axes provided.

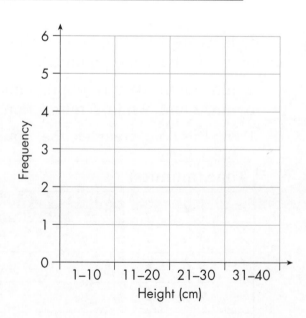

Exercise 16B Mode, median and range

This exercise will give you practice in

o finding the mode, the median and the range for small sets of data

1 Find the mode and the range of each of the following sets of data.

a 2   4   4   5   7   7   7   8   8   10

Mode = _____   Range = _____

b 1   1   1   3   6   6   8   9   9   10

Mode = _____   Range = _____

c 12   12   15   15   16   17   20   20   20   20

Mode = _____   Range = _____

2 Order the sets of data from smallest to largest, and then find the mode and the range of each set.

a   3   6   4   9   8   1   2   4   9   4

____   ____   ____   ____   ____   ____   ____   ____   ____   ____

Mode = _____   Range = _____

b   17   12   12   4   18   17   11   10   12

____   ____   ____   ____   ____   ____   ____   ____   ____

Mode = _____   Range = _____

3 Find the median of each of the following sets of data.

a 2   4   7   7   8   10   11   11   11   Median = _____

b 15   18   18   19   22   24   25   Median = _____

c 25   28   28   31   32   36   37   Median = _____

4 Order the sets of data from smallest to largest, and then find the median.

a   8   3   4   6   7

____   ____   ____   ____   ____   Median = _____

b   14   11   13   16   15

____   ____   ____   ____   ____   Median = _____

5 Find the mode, the median and the range for the following sets of data.
Remember to put the data in order of size first.

a £2 £13 £3 £16 £22 £7 £8 £2 £1

_____ _____ _____ _____ _____ _____ _____ _____ _____

Mode = _____ Range = _____ Median = _____

b 10 cm 5 cm 4 cm 4 cm 14 cm 2 cm 6 cm

_____ _____ _____ _____ _____ _____ _____

Mode = _____ Range = _____ Median = _____

Exercise 16C Calculating means

This exercise will give you practice in

o calculating the mean for small sets of data

1 Calculate the mean for each of the following sets of data. Use the formula:

$$\text{Mean} = \frac{\text{Sum of all values in the set}}{\text{Number of values in the set}}$$

a 1 2 3 4 5   **b** 1 8 1 2

Mean = ——— = _____   Mean = ——— = _____

_____   _____

c 6 4 5 5   **d** 7 3 9 1 4 6 2 8 10 5

Mean = ——— = _____   Mean = ——— = _____

_____   _____

2 Calculate the mean for each of the following sets of data. Use the formula:

$$\text{Mean} = \frac{\text{Sum of all values in the set}}{\text{Number of values in the set}}$$

a 12 32 34 45 52   **b** 12 83 14 23

Mean = ——— = _____   Mean = ——— = _____

_____   _____

c 64 47 51 58

Mean = ——————— = ——————

d 27 91 13 39 70

Mean = ——————— = ——————

(3) The spending money of 12 children is:

£3   £5   £10   £4.50   £3.50   £5   £4.50   £7.50   £10   £5   £7.50   £6.50

a Calculate the mean amount of spending money. ——————————

b How many children get more than the mean amount? ——————————

(4) 10 students estimate the size of an angle. Their estimates are given below.

30°   40°   30°   55°   60°   20°   50°   45°   25°   40°

a Calculate the mean of the estimates. ——————————

b The correct size of the angle is an exact multiple of 10, for example 10°, 20° and so on. Use your mean to estimate the exact angle.

Exercise 16D Averages

This exercise will give you practice in

o   knowing which average to use

(1) Look at each of the examples in the table on the next page and decide which average is the most useful. Explain your answer.

		Most useful average	Reason
a	Average shoe size	Mean (= 5.6) or mode (= 6)	
b	Test results of 5 pupils all with different scores	Mean or mode	
c	Average contents of a packet of biscuits	Median (= 18) or mean (= 18.3)	
d	Average height of 14-year olds	Mean or mode	
e	Average dress size	Median or mean	
f	Average number of wheels per vehicle	Mode or mean	
g	Average number of people in a boy band	Mode or mean	

2 Raj wants to survey how students in his class travel to school. Should he use the mode, the median or the mean to comment on his results? Explain your answer.

_____

_____

_____

3 Jake carries out a survey on how much people earn. Should he use the mode, the median or the mean to comment on his results? Explain your answer.

_____

_____

_____

Exercise 16E Statistical surveys

This exercise will give you practice in
- carrying out a statistical survey

(1) Choose one of the following topics to investigate, or choose a topic of your own.

A   The amount of television watched by secondary school students. (Does the amount of televison watched affect the amount of time spent on homework?)

B   Favourite types of music. (Which type of music is the most popular?)

C   The amount of exercise people take. (Do boys do more exercise than girls?)

D   Students' favourite sports. (Taking part in or watching. Do you get different answers?)

Topic to investigate: _____

Before you carry out your survey, complete the following table.

Question	Answer
How big will my sample be? For example, how many people will I survey?	
Where will I carry out my survey? For example, will I ask people in my class or friends outside of school?	
Am I going to use a questionnaire or a data collection sheet? For example, will I use a set of short questions with tick boxes or will I use a tally chart to collect my data together?	
Will I put my results in a table or a diagram? For example, will I draw a bar chart?	
What is my conclusion? For example, what can I conclude from my investigation based on my results?	

Now carry out your survey and comment on your results. Use A4 paper.

Exercise 16F Using the results from an experiment

This exercise will give you practice in

○ using results from an experiment

① Choose one of the following experiments, or choose an experiment of your own.

A   Roll a dice many times to decide if it is biased (not fair).

B   Flip a coin many times to decide if it is biased.

Experiment to investigate: _____

Before you carry out your experiment, complete the following table.

Question	Answer
How big will my sample be? For example, how many times will I roll the dice?	
How will I record my results? For example, will I use a tally chart and frequency table?	
Will I calculate experimental probabilities? For example, 25 heads out of 40 flips = $\frac{25}{40}$	
What is my conclusion? For example, is the coin biased? Explain my conclusion.	

Now carry out your experiment. Record your results and conclusions on A4 paper.

Published by Collins
An imprint of HarperCollins*Publishers*
77–85 Fulham Palace Road
Hammersmith
London
W6 8JB

Browse the complete Collins catalogue at
www.collinseducation.com

© HarperCollins*Publishers* Limited 2008

10 9 8 7

ISBN-13 978-0-00-726797-2

Trevor Senior asserts his moral right to be identified as the author
of this work.

All rights reserved. No part of this publication may be
reproduced, stored in a retrieval system, or transmitted in any
form or by any means, electronic, mechanical, photocopying,
recording or otherwise, without the prior written permission of the
Publisher or a licence permitting restricted copying in the United
Kingdom issued by the Copyright Licensing Agency Ltd., 90
Tottenham Court Road, London W1T 4LP.

British Library Cataloguing in Publication Data
A Catalogue record for this publication is available from the
British Library.

Commissioned by Katie Sergeant
Design and typesetting by Newgen
Edited by Karen Westall
Project managed by Sue Chapple
Proofread by Margaret Shepherd
Illustrations by Nigel Jordan and Tony Wilkins
Covers by Oculus Design and Communications
Production by Simon Moore
Printed and bound by Printing Express, Hong Kong

Every effort has been made to trace copyright holders and to
obtain their permission for the use of copyright material. The
authors and publishers will gladly receive any information
enabling them to rectify any error or omission in subsequent
editions.

Mixed Sources
Product group from well-managed
forests and other controlled sources
www.fsc.org Cert no. SW-COC-001806
© 1996 Forest Stewardship Council
FSC

FSC is a non-profit international organisation established to promote the
responsible management of the world's forests. Products carrying the FSC
label are independently certified to assure consumers that they come
from forests that are managed to meet the social, economic and
ecological needs of present and future generations.

Find out more about HarperCollins and the environment at
www.harpercollins.co.uk/green